POETRY C

GREAT MINDS

Your World...Your Future...YOUR WORDS

From Near And Far

Edited by Steve Twelvetree

 Young**Writers**

First published in Great Britain in 2005 by:
Young Writers
Remus House
Coltsfoot Drive
Peterborough
PE2 9JX
Telephone: 01733 890066
Website: www.youngwriters.co.uk

SB ISBN 1 84602 211 8

Foreword

This year, the Young Writers' 'Great Minds' competition proudly presents a showcase of the best poetic talent selected from over 40,000 up-and-coming writers nationwide.

Young Writers was established in 1991 to promote the reading and writing of poetry within schools and to the youth of today. Our books nurture and inspire confidence in the ability of young writers and provide a snapshot of poems written in schools and at home by budding poets of the future.

The thought, effort, imagination and hard work put into each poem impressed us all and the task of selecting poems was a difficult but nevertheless enjoyable experience.

We hope you are as pleased as we are with the final selection and that you and your family continue to be entertained with *Great Minds From Near And Far* for many years to come.

Contents

Sarah Roche (13)   18

City of Preston High School, Preston
Terri Gregson (13)   18
Chelsea Sanders (12)   19
Leigh Harrison (12)   19
Katie Ryan (15)   20
Kirsty Fisher (12)   21
Daniel Dickinson (13)   22

Dubai College, United Arab Emirates
Kalyani Nedungadi (13)   23
Fiona Tarbet (12)   24

Hawick High School, Hawick
Andrew King (13)   25
Rory Anderson (13)   25
Philip Mactaggart (13)   26
Craig Bell (13)   26
Megan Gracie (14)   27
Rebecca Lee (13)   28
Mairi Cameron (13)   29
Mark Graham (14)   30
Ashley Drysdale (13)   30
Sarah Thompson (13)   31
James McPherson (14)   31
Gillian Hogg (14)   32
Caitlin Hamilton (13)   33
Greg Stark (13)   34
Lois Niblo (13)   34
Kieran Willison (13)   35
Jak Scott (13)   35
Jaimie Nichol (14)   36
Toni Pearce (12)   36

Inverness Royal Academy, Inverness
Emma Atkinson (12)   37
Aysa Basbayraktar (13)   38
Gary James Paterson (13)   38
Lauren Cormack (13)   39

Danielle Henderson (14)   63
Gillian McGlashan (13)   64
Max Newcombe   65
Stephanie Armstrong   66
Raymond Hill (13)   67
Jennifer Kerr (13)   68
Kirsty Stewart   69
Jamie Balfour (13)   70
Amanda Veal   71
Daniel McNeill   72

Rushcliffe School, Nottingham
Thomas Slapp (12)   72
Gurjeet Roth (13)   73
Daniel Sutherland (13)   73
Antonio Barlow (13)   74
Felicity Cooper (12)   74
Harley Greener (12)   75
Ellen Malone (13)   75
Flossie Eyden (13)   76
Jade Cito (12)   76
Holly Wain (13)   77
Vicki Clark (12)   78
Sam Price (12)   78
Alistair Britton (12)   79
Dominic Lowes (13)   79
Paige Wilson (12)   80

St Louis Grammar School, Ballymena
Alan Barr (14)   81
Emma Dooey (12)   82
Shona O'Rawe (14)   82

St Luke's High School, Barrhead
Christopher Docherty (13)   83
Peter McAllister (12)   83
Fern Maxwell (12)   83
Laura McDonald (12)   84
Megan McBride (12)   84
Martyn Wilson (13)   85
Kayleigh McPherson (13)   85

Jane Lunday (13)	86
Dominic Mercer (12)	86
Lauren Heaney (12)	87

St Nicholas Catholic High School, Northwich

Helen O'Brien (13)	87
Scott Prince (11)	88
Emily-May Walker (11)	88
Emma Phillips (11)	89
Grace Wells (11)	90
Grace Ashcroft (11)	90
Lauren Stanton (11)	91
Annabelle Keaveny (11)	91
Rachael Williams (11)	92
Samantha Roe (13)	93
Alex Willemsen (11)	94
Gabriella Gough (11)	95
Andrew Jones (11)	95
Matthew Whittaker (11)	96

San Silvestre School, Peru

Aarti Daryanani (13)	96
Angie Hanawa (12)	97
Maria Laura Lizarzaburu (16)	98

Stewarton Academy, Stewarton

Johnathan Walker	99
Joe Stubbs (12)	99
Stephen Shaw (12)	99
Emma Milligan (13)	100
Christopher Dinning (12)	100
Matthew Allison (12)	101
Alistair Green (12)	101
Colin Stapely (13)	101
Emily Poggi	102
Paul Stephen (12)	102
Robbie McCreadie (12)	102
Gordon Burnett (13)	103
Blair Smith (12)	103
Ewan Baillie (12)	104
Kirsty McWilliam (12)	104

Conor Nisbet (12)   105
Rachel Bow (12)   105
Rachael Sheach (12)   106
Lindsay Richmond (12)   106
Greg Leyden (12)   107
Briony Mitchell (12)   107
Darren Ronaldson (12)   108
Ruairidh McMillan (12)   108
Caitlin Burns (12)   109

Stratford-upon-Avon High School, Stratford-upon-Avon

Laura Marszalek (12)   110
Louie Kenyon-Crockett (13)   111
Bethan Jones (13)   112
Alice Kinoulty (12)   112
Christina Mann (13)   113
Stuart Macaulay (13)   113
Chloe Guy (13)   114
Ben Parry (13)   115
Charlotte Howdle (13)   116
Louisa Heyworth (13)   116
Emma Stubbs (12)   117
Zoe Lucock (12)   118
Victoria Lyon (13)   119
Gabby May (12)   120
Pete Hurst (13)   121

The King's Academy, Middlesbrough

Thomas Barron (12)   121
Laura Noble (12)   122
Alyssa Bodycombe (13)   122
Matthew Kirby (13)   123
Ben Nixon (12)   123
Alexandra Miller (12)   124
Amy B Bell (12)   124
Sarah Pinkney (12)   125
Eleanor Trueman (12)   125
Louise McGill (12)   126
Bethany Elenor (12)   127
Katie Leggett (12)   128
Perry Frost (12)   128

The Meadows School, Coventry

Chris Clarke (13)   158
Shay Oliver (14)   159
Jamie Worwood (15)   160
Philip Ball (15)   161
Josh Nagle (12)   162
Adam Johnson (12)   162
Jamie Braithwaite (14)   163
Matthew Griffiths (14)   164

The Nottingham Emmanuel School, Nottingham
Claire Waring (12)   164
Tom Mason (12)   165
Daniella Binch (13)   165
Seonaid Beaumont (12)   166
Luke Derby (13)   166
Jamie Buchan (13)   167
Rory Devonport (13)   167
Emma Upton (13)   168
Simon Verhoeven (12)   169
Chris Ford   170
Lois Brown (13)   171
Kelly Ridley (12)   172
Emma Boulton (13)   173
Daniel Flint (13)   174
Daniel Neville (13)   175
George Gadd (13)   176
Ellis Dunkley (13)   177
Matt Slater (13)   178

The Ralph Sadleir School, Puckeridge
Cara Neale   178
Charlotte Marro (11)   179
Amy Carter (11)   179
George Cook (11)   180
Becky Bird (11)   180
Chloe Fox (11)   181
Heather Gillam   181
Jourdana Fairlie (11)   182
James Backham (11)   182
Natasha Mead   183
Josh Davies (11)   183

Sam Deville (11)	184
Georgia Higgins (11)	185
Robyn Turner	185
Aimée Jeromson (11)	186
Kate Davies	186
Eveigh Noble (11)	187
Sara Gilbert (11)	187
Lana Premadasa	188
Bianca Burridge (11)	188
Charlotte Kearley (11)	189
Oliver Kerr (11)	189
Catherine Sheridan (11)	190
Peter Dalton (11)	190
Sarah Jackson (11)	191
Robert England (11)	191
Shauni Barrett (11)	192
Steven Fredericks (11)	192
Charlotte Williams (11)	193
Thomas Santurri (11)	193
Rufus Pratt	193
Jasmin Geddes-Rainbow (11)	194
Gillian Gibbons (11)	194
Tom Jeffries (11)	195
James Danter (11)	195

Tottington High School, Bury

Catherine Keene (13)	196
Katie Eves (13)	197
Lea Taylor (13)	198
Sam Winstanley (13)	199
Annabelle Kelly (13)	200
Melissa Butterworth (13)	201
Gabriella Sloss (13)	202
Victoria Hinde (13)	203
Adam Dickinson (12)	204
Becky Foulkes (12)	205
Sophie Mather (13)	206
Andrew Fairclough (13)	207
Rachel Thomas (13)	208
Robert Dennis (13)	209
Hannah Price (13)	210

Kirstie Bailey (13)   211
James Kidd (13)   212
Edward Robson (13)   213
Hayley Driver (13)   214
Naomi Tod (13)   215
Luke Aspinall (13)   216
Leanne Savery (13)   217
Jessica Brindle (13)   218

Wareham Middle School, Wareham
Paul Edwards (12)   218
Sarah Thomas (12)   219
Michael Alberry (12)   219
Danielle Burbidge   220
James Drane (13)   220
Harry Ward   221
Kara Birch   221
Sophie Bellingham (13)   222
Kieran Taylor   222
April Parslow (13)   223
Gabriella Mytton-Mills (12)   223

Westwood St Thomas' School, Salisbury
Roxanne Baker (13)   224
Danielle Cotsell (14)   224
Koby Waters (14)   225
Holly Turner (14)   225
Brierly Keeton (14)   226
Lisa Shearmon (14)   226
Laura Stokes (14)   227
Sophie Astley (14)   227
Angelia Ferris (14)   228
Holly Clarke (14)   228
Delith Morton (13)   229
Helen Grinter (14)   229

Woodlands Special High School, Cardiff
Kenneth Marshall (17)   230
Jonathan Bryant (18)   230

The Poems

Through My Eyes

Ahead I see a future of happiness
Where the dictator is peace, and
The rulers are love and friendship.
Loneliness, pain, combined with all hate
Are history lessons in which our children fall asleep.

In the mirror I see a dreamer,
Young, insignificant and all her power still to show.
For I am the future,
I am the ruler ahead.
I have so much to become
And so many choices to make.
I will rule using love and friendship,
I will dictate peace.
It is I who is the dreamer.
I see the dream.

Nicole Phillips (16)

Love

Love is something you feel,
A feeling of deep emotion.
Love is something you give,
To people you care about.
Love is something you receive,
From people that care about you.
Love is when you feel all nice inside,
Like everything will turn out right,
Like butterflies inside you.
Love is what I feel,
For the people that I love.

Lauren Bambrough (15)
Ashington Community High School Sports College, Ashington

You

Lifeless as a corpse,
Meaningless as a kiss,
Heartless as the world,
Are you hearing this?
Feeling less like the wind,
Heartless like a bruise,
Spiritless like a bird,
Why are you making me choose?
I have nothing in this life,
I have no meaning too,
As my heart beats I hear -
But I'm not hearing you!
I feel so empty here,
I feel pain and anger too,
As my spirit drifts away,
I will, I have chosen you!

Leonie Reed (15)
Ashington Community High School Sports College, Ashington

Toni's Sonnet

The one I love his hair so soft and blond,
His eyes are a deep blue, glistening pond,
His full, dark lips so gentle and so sweet,
He's like air to my breath, shoes to my feet,
His smooth caress, the feeling it gives me,
His light scent a subtle ghost I can't see,
The whisper in his voice so warm and true,
The twinkle in his eye like morning dew,
He has crystal tears and a firm embrace,
A welcoming smile that lights up his face,
We're shaped by other's reactions to us,
It's love, I adore all he says and does,
I wrote this poem so he knows I care
About the kisses, hugs and tears we share.

Antonia Edwards (14)
Ashington Community High School Sports College, Ashington

Can't Forget, No Regrets

Once you were there so beautiful
I had to remind myself that this was real
You were so great to me, so loyal and dutiful
You made me believe in love
You taught me how to feel

But like most good things it was not to be
Now you're gone as if you never cared
Did you ever look back? Did you see?
I don't think that you ever knew
I allowed myself to love you. Why had I dared?

Tears fell and then they were no more
I got angry and then turned sad
Others would move on but my heart is still sore
I still think of you, every little word
Why was it not enough, what we had?

Every little kiss and every touch
Every time I saw you, every time we met
Brought with its warmth so much
How could you leave me for all those mindless girls?
You placed both our lives on a poor odds bet

You said you loved us
But of course you only meant that you got a kick
You only meant teenage lust
Why the hell was I so stupid?
Things you said about me, bet they even made you sick

I believe you only get one chance
One person in life that matters
Would I ever give you a second glance?
You were meant but no, now I have nothing
My world lies broken in love's uncanny tatters

I can never love because I'm broken
I can never truly feel
In my thoughts until I am woken
I hope the world will learn
Isn't love a never-ending deal?

Lyndsey Graham (14)
Ashington Community High School Sports College, Ashington

Becca's Poem

If she were an animal she'd be a kitten,
Warm and cuddly like a fluffy mitten.
If she were a colour she would be pink,
Standing out in a crowd like a tropical drink.
If she were the weather she'd be the sun,
Running beside you on your hot, summer's run.
If she were an element she'd be the air,
Always around you no matter where.
If she were furniture she'd be a pillow,
Snuggling you in when you're a weeping willow.
If she were a drink she'd be orange juice,
Quenching your thirst with a burst of fruit.
If she were food she'd be chips with tomato sauce,
Everyone likes her, and them of course.
If she were a movie she'd be comedy,
Always game for a laugh and she's not just anybody.
If she were clothing she'd be a white fur coat,
Stylish and soft, always wanting to gloat.
If she were a smell she'd be a rose,
Known to others as a smell on your clothes.
If she were a number she would be seven,
An age she didn't get to before she went to Heaven.

Sarah Louise Watson (14)
Ashington Community High School Sports College, Ashington

Diving Bird

Rare and expansive,
The last of its kind,
Swiftly it shaves the air and sea.

The endless fields of blue,
The wheat deadly cold,
The home for many, for now.

Born strong and noble,
Held in highest respect,
Its feathers are gold and white.

Yet gentle,
Its muscle dying,
Its heart alive forever.

The struggle continues,
Ahead lies an end,
Shock befell those who suffered and the bird.

This bird fell,
The ocean cold,
With it memory, of people dear.

And through people dear,
The diving bird, will live.

Adam Joseph Marsden (13)
Bedford Modern School, Bedford

My Mind

My mind floats like a leaf in this wicked air,
With nowhere to fall and with no thoughts to care.
My mind lies awake and trembles all alone,
When I can't sleep at night its silence is its drone.
My mind is alive but it feels so cold,
It is unfulfilled like a man with no soul.
My mind lies awake and not once I have dreamed,
With a whole world to explore that not once I have seen.
My mind cannot grow, it's barren of ideas,
It's like not being able to hear but having twelve ears.
My mind is a painful recreation without the memories,
It's like a sprawling battlefield without the enemies.
My mind tries to set my soul a bursting heat of fire,
With no passion whatsoever to fill my heart's desire.
My mind is my mind however it seems,
My mind is a safekeeping locked in my dreams.

Joeben Nassereslam (15)
Bedford Modern School, Bedford

Embers

Echoes of a broken child burn through the air,
Screams of women flow from smoke-filled craters,
And no one seems to care.

Blinding light seers from nearby blasts,
Which kill thousands in their wake,
The rancid stench of death and destruction,
Which causes so much heartache.

Men and women fighting for a cause which is no longer just,
Belief and faith is lost to them, now all they have is trust.

Gunshots ring throughout the darkness, hitting every target,
Images of horrific bloodshed create scenes one can never forget.

So as the rest of us rot in passive fertility,
Inexperienced and unaware,
Giving orders and making demands, think! Is this fair?

Craig Knox (15)
Bedford Modern School, Bedford

The Life Within These Walls

The life within these walls, my dear,
Is very dark and stuffy.
The life within these walls, my dear,
Makes me cold and hungry.

If you come inside, my dear,
You'll see a hellish sight.
If you come inside, my dear,
You'll see our horrible plight.

If you follow me, my dear,
Watch your purse and head.
Because if you don't, my dear,
You're bound to end up dead.

Now join me for lunch, my dear,
We're having rats again.
But if you refuse, you'll join the queue
And never be seen again!

Matthew Wong (13)
Bedford Modern School, Bedford

The Statue

It stands there, silent as a grave,
Solid and still,
Its immovable arms,
Wish all who see it ill.

Its cold, dead eyes,
Look into your soul,
Rip through your heart,
And leave you unwhole.

Its muted lips,
Speak words to your mind,
Tell you to crush the good,
And let evil unbind.

It stands there, silent as a grave,
But in its silence,
The path of darkness to pave.

Stephen Hartill (13)
Bedford Modern School, Bedford

Hope

Hope is yellow
It smells like the first
Daffodil in spring
It tastes like sweet porridge
On a cold, winter's morning
It feels like a relaxing bath
After a hard day
Hope lives in
Every little baby.

Shay Horner (14)
Belmont School, Cheltenham

Dreams And Reality

It's England v France
89 minutes gone and it's 0-0
Then I get the ball
I skin all the French players including Zinedine Zidane
I'm one-on-one with the goalkeeper
And I place it in the top right-hand corner of the goal.

Tap, tap . . .

My mum has woken me up
To get ready for school
The reality is I'll have to dream the rest tonight.

Dean Lockey (16)
Belmont School, Cheltenham

Purple Helmets

I am going down the motorway
On my brand new motorbike.
A lorry comes up behind me cutting me up.
The wind is blowing against my helmet.
What a great life, then
I fall off . . . *ouch!*

Suddenly I am busy at school.
The teacher's voice is going on and on . . .
Then the teacher asks me a question.
I don't know the answer
Because I am daydreaming.

Gavin Powles (15)
Belmont School, Cheltenham

Slowly My Heart Begins To Pound . . .

Slowly my heart begins to pound
I can feel my heart racing
I try not to make a sound
What can I do?

The hours seem to draw by closer
I hide myself in the darkness
Why don't I ever stop feeling sorrow and pain?
Will I be stronger and win this battle, this game?

My heart screams
What can I say?
I feel worried if I don't get stronger and be a loser.
So I try to stop thinking about the comments people have said.

So I put a smile on my face
Thinking of a happy place
Where I'd like to be.
I am a winner and a good friend
I should be able to see.

So the next day
I toughen myself up
And tell myself I'm a winner.
Now people can see how I see myself, as someone, something
Even though I'm a beginner.

So I wipe out my unhappiness
And be a stronger, happier person
So I stop thinking about sadness
And think of gladness.

I won't ever feel this sad again
And I won't dwell on what happens
I am a winner, not a loser
And if people can't see this
Then they're really not worth it.

We will have rights and independence
I won't let sad and pathetic people bring me down.
I can be whatever I want to be.
If people frown at who I am,
Then let them frown.

Katie Johnson (15)
Belmont School, Cheltenham

Better Than Life

I am in my tank
With a Gatling gun in my hands.
The smell of my enemies,
Fear on the tip of my tongue,
Then my stomach tumbles.

'KO!'

A loud voice shouts out.
It is my computer game.
I must have fallen asleep while
I was playing the game.
Oh no, have just lost my game.

Oh well, that dream was better than life!

Brendon Herbert (15)
Belmont School, Cheltenham

Dreams And Reality

On a Monday morning I have my new tractor driving in the fields.
The door is open and the cool air is running through the cab.
The farm smell is in the air.
The rabbits are running along the hedgerows.
It is a wonderful life.

'Darren, Darren, stop daydreaming . . .'
I am at school.
The teacher is gabbling on to us,
I can smell the sweat of a busy classroom,
I am a long way from home!

Darren Scrivens (15)
Belmont School, Cheltenham

My Life

When I'm alone, I wonder why,
I've been left alone, to just sit and cry.
No one likes me, and no one cares,
About my feelings like they're not there.

I hate my life, it's such a mess,
Everyone hates me, and the way I dress.
Maybe it's time to leave my life,
Open the drawer and get the knife.

I wonder what everyone'll think,
When I kick the bucket, wash away
Down the sink.

So this is it, I'm gonna do it,
Get the knife, smile the whole way
Through it.

Goodbye world,
Goodbye me.
I bet you don't believe me,
But soon you'll see . . .

Amy Osborne (13)
Bridgewater School, Berkhamsted

The Mansion Of Forgotten Dreams

The crumbling steps
The jagged door
The smashed windows
The bloodstained floor
The axe that hangs above the fire
Many souls did here expire
The chilling cries
The haunting jeers
The shouts of death
And long-lost fears
The mansion of forgotten dreams
The dead lie waiting for your screams
The last mistake they ever made;
The house they bought
The price they paid.

Ben Michel (11)
Bridgewater School, Berkhamsted

What Is Bullying?

Bullying is insults sparkling like fluorescent fireworks,
Flowing in a circle of hate.
They erupt from the mouth and burn through the ear,
And torture the innocent brain.

Bullying is forcing like the wind in your face,
On a frosty, winter's day.
Bullying forces the dinner money,
Bullying is like being possessed - a force against your will.

Bullying is pain like a quick, sharp, metal beat,
Rapidly hurting everything, making your body tingle.
Bullying is like an earthquake, shaking, jingling your body.
Bullying is wrong.

Harry Lee
Bridgewater School, Berkhamsted

Waiting For Summer

Rain, thunder, lightning so bright,
A storm so dangerous on this summer night.
Wind, wind so very strong,
What is it lasting so long?
Trees and flowers all blown away,
No beauty to see this certain day.
How will the day be tomorrow,
Am I going to suffer in sorrow?
Rain flooded this particular street,
From my knees down to my feet.
Would this rain stop at all?
So far the storm stands tall.

Huseyin Hodja (11)
Bridgewater School, Berkhamsted

At The Zoo

At the zoo
There were apples falling
Babies bawling
Lions roaring
Larks soaring
There were boys and girls talking
Parrots squawking
Dogs growling
Wolves howling
There were rabbits munching
Families lunching
Zebras grazing
The sun was blazing
There were hummingbirds humming
And more people coming.

Tim Warr
Bridgewater School, Berkhamsted

Devil's River

Wind whistles through the leaves,
The bravest of birds don't venture near,
Hills, valleys all bleak and forlorn,
Through the hazy veil of rain.

The river bursts its banks with a roar,
Water pounds and cascades in fountains,
Vast seas and oceans seem small and sweet,
Compared to Devil's River.

Big towns and cities are engulfed,
Woods and fields are sent choking for air,
Invading streams and smaller rivers,
Nothing escapes the slaughter.

People scream and flee for their lives,
'The Devil's curse!' they cry in fear,
Father, Mother, all the locals,
Panicking, cursing they run.

Devil's River, don't go near it,
Not even the bravest visit,
Saints can never speak good of it,
It's the faithful hound of Satan.

Sian Johnson (11)
Bridgewater School, Berkhamsted

Our World

Sky of blue
Sea of green
Sun of gold
And pansies cream.

World of wonder
Stars in space
Objects sold
In every place.

Fish of fins
Birds of wings
Humans of legs
And tiny things.

Carrots orange
Strawberries sweet
Summer berries
And home-grown wheat.

Sunny holidays
Sandy shores
Little crabs
With mini claws.

This is our world
As a world should be
Excitement and fun
In everything we see.

Sophie Edwards (11)
Bridgewater School, Berkhamsted

Venus

Named in honour of the goddess of beauty and love
This planet can be seen from above
Named the morning and evening star
Venus is beauty from afar

From the sun it is number two
And women being there is very true
Lisa, Diana and Guinevere
Each one is a name for a surface feature

It once had water but has no moon
Probes sent there are crushed all too soon
Similar to Earth in mass and size
But Earth life on Venus would all die

The hottest planet in the night
It keeps the sun's heat and reflects its light
A rocky planet with a dense atmosphere
Of the acid rain you must keep clear

Volcanoes, dry rocks and a surface that glows
What's really on Venus no one knows
Carbon dioxide thick in the air
This corrosive planet can be hard to bear

Venus' year is longer than its day
And from the Earth it turns a different way
Going clockwise, known as the bringer of peace
The sun rises in the west and sets in the east.

Becky Scott (12)
Bridgewater School, Berkhamsted

Haiku

A fox that is red
With a white end on the tail
Goes out in the night.

Jonathan Daly (13)
Brookfields School, Widnes

Sun

In the night-time the sunset goes down
And when it goes down it is red sky of the sun.
Then it's cool when the sun is down
And when it comes out the next day it is fun.

Aaron Jennion (17)
Brookfields School, Widnes

Haiku

Names can be funny
Sometimes they are used to skit
They can be quite sad.

Sarah Roche (13)
Brookfields School, Widnes

I Should Not Have Said Goodbye

I look so deeply into the mirror
And see my little sister's killer.
I shed a little tear
Because I have so much fear.

I hold your picture so close to my heart
I never wanted us to be apart
Because you're my little sister
And I know I miss you.

You didn't deserve to die
I hope you know I cry.
I stand at your grave,
I try to be brave.

I just wanted to let you know
That I do love you so.

Terri Gregson (13)
City of Preston High School, Preston

School Poem

My favourite lesson is IT
And it's all about me.
I hate all the boys
Who play with baby toys.

Mr Ward is sound
While the kids are around.
He lets us have free time
When the choice is mine.

Mr Whiteside is strict
But only for a bit.
He shouts and screams
And that's so mean.

Mr Carefoot can be kind
But only in his own mind.
We do all the work that is set
Otherwise Mr Carefoot will be upset.

Chelsea Sanders (12)
City of Preston High School, Preston

My Love

My love for you is deeper than the deepest ocean.
My love for you is like a stream that never ends.
My love for you is more than you will ever know.
But your eyes are like sapphires
Your cheeks are like roses.
When you speak it's like a tune
That's being sung by angels.
Your hair is like a shiny piece of gold.
Well, my love, I have to go
But do not forget I love you!
I will always be with you in your heart.

Leigh Harrison (12)
City of Preston High School, Preston

Macbeth

One man's ambition,
To defy the laws of fate,
At a time of transparent murder,
Of treason and of hate.

The lives that did surround him,
Destroyed when in his path.
A swirling pool of mastermind,
A raging, bleak bloodbath.

Absorbed inside his evil,
So much he can't elope.
Entangled in a web of lies,
He found he could not cope.

Once a man of courage,
With honour, hope and dream,
Now a man of emptiness,
With nothing so it seems.

His undying soul now shackled,
In chains of crime and death.
Eternal pain would meet him,
This man they call Macbeth.

Katie Ryan   (15)
City of Preston High School, Preston

My School

Welcome to City of Preston High,
It's the best school and I'll tell you why,
The teachers are cool, the lessons are great,
There's nobody here that I hate.

Mrs Palmer's PE is such a scream,
I can't stop laughing on the trampoline,
But science and history can be boring,
Sometimes I feel a bit like snoring.

Mrs Stewart sometimes lets us play games,
But I work very hard to get good grades,
And there's Mr Carefoot who teaches art,
He's very good and always looks smart.

Mr Ward is funny and I like him the best,
Because he makes me laugh more than the rest,
So that's the story of my school,
And the reasons that I think it's cool.

Kirsty Fisher (12)
City of Preston High School, Preston

The Monster

I was in my bed fast asleep
Then I suddenly heard a little beep.
I woke up to look around
But nothing was there, not a sound.
I went back to sleep because nothing was there
I looked back up and there it were.

It was huge and it was green,
It was so terribly mean and mean
It was awful and made me scream.

It had 6 eyes and had 10 toes
And had 5 arms but had no nose.
It had razor-sharp teeth that it was grinding
There was no weapon that I was finding.

I was so scared and was terribly shaking
It is no lie, I am not faking.
I tried to scream again but nothing came out
Until I cried and let out a terrible shout.

Then it ate me and gobbled me up
So very fast it had a hiccup.
There was blood on the window and blood on the bed
As it shoved its fingers into its big, fat head.

And that's the end of my small life
I didn't live up to have a wife.
Instead I'm in the greasy belly
Of the most ugliest monster on the telly!

Daniel Dickinson (13)
City of Preston High School, Preston

The Silent Snow Leopard

A snowy night - a blizzard rages;
Everyone trapped in their homes - in cages.
Everyone, except the silent snow leopard.

Sleekly moving, ice-patched pelt,
Under guard fur - cold, barely felt.
Moves the silent snow leopard.

An art in itself with spot embroidered fur.
Incapable of roar; a modest purr.
Long tail a scarf, padded paws are shoes;
Sure-footed in the barest crack of a groove.
Sounds the silent snow leopard.

In the tallest Himalayas at nineteen thousand feet,
In a summer of barest heat,
Musk deer, wild sheep, hares, mice;
Find themselves in the vice-like grip of ice.
Hunts the silent snow leopard.

Elusive and shy, solitary and quiet;
No picture could match the splendour of it.
Its leaps are long, its jumps are high,
Watchful eyes reach for the sky.
Bounds the silent snow leopard.

A covering of ice, a mind of fire,
Ready to pounce - a coiled-up wire.
Body of grace, teeth of death;
Each kill thought through but scarcely felt.
Lives the silent snow leopard.

The hunter of hunters, the lord of the mountain,
It is, and has been and so will his kin.
But now more are prey and find themselves poached,
By malice-bearing farmers or arrogance wanting coats.
Now cattle feel safe, not a predator in sight,
All enemies are gone with the night.
All enemies except that of the silent snow leopard.

Kalyani Nedungadi (13)
Dubai College, United Arab Emirates

In February

In February
The rollers fly by
With their blue breasts
A salute to the sky.

A few duck low
To catch naïve toads
Noticing but a turquoise flash
As they laze on dusty roads.

They reach a clearing
Their bodies a-gleam
Inspecting their purple necks
And blue breasts waiting to be seen.

A screech and then
Begins a dance
That is a desperate struggle
For romance.

They fly up through the air
Like a plane first taking flight
And tumble down
As if struck with might.

They screech and flap
Their wings during flight.
A battle unfolds,
A battle for the spotlight.

In the end one by one
They pair off and leave
Until there is nothing
But the sound of the breeze.

Fiona Tarbet (12)
Dubai College, United Arab Emirates

Snowy, Snowy Day

It's started snowing again.
Will it get heavy?
Probably.
Maybe.
Hopefully . . .

What's that?
Snowball!
Curled up hedgehog.
Pounding my ear.
Leaving only the icy needles.

Are my ears hot or cold?
I can't feel my toes.
My fingers are ice cubes.
My ears are the snow.
I should have worn my hat.

My ears are sorer than pulling teeth.
My hands are soaked.
What shall I do?
This snow is lava . . .
I'm going home.

Andrew King (13)
Hawick High School, Hawick

The Pen

The pen is a soldier standing to attention
Ready to fight his way along the line
It is a spear pinning words to paper
Struggling to break free.
The paper is a battlefield
Covered with dead words
It is a sheet of snow
Stained black and blue.

Rory Anderson (13)
Hawick High School, Hawick

The Sea Is . . .

The sea is . . .
A shark's fridge,
An endless, blue carpet,
Nemo's house,
A blue, leaking pen.
The sea is . . .
Never dry,
A lion's roar,
A seal's playground,
A water park.
The sea is . . .
God's tears,
Sadness,
An unexplored wonder,
Someone's imagination.
The sea is . . .
A tap someone forgot to turn off,
A fisherman's dream,
A giant puddle,
A predator.
The sea is . . .
A killer.

Philip Mactaggart (13)
Hawick High School, Hawick

Poem

The teacher ran her nails down the blackboard.
It sounded awful, like a million things,
A car slamming its brakes on,
A knife cutting a stone,
Children screaming constantly,
A high-pitched alarm squealing for help,
A baby crying in the night,
But most of all nails going down a blackboard.

Craig Bell (13)
Hawick High School, Hawick

Personality

What does it look like?
It looks like - the burning sun,
The fluffy clouds,
The calm, blue sea,
Heaven.

What does it sound like?
It sounds like - laughing, crying,
Shouting, whispering,
Silence.

What does it taste like?
It tastes like - curry, yoghurt,
Fruit or veg,
Nothing.

What does it feel like?
It feels like cotton wool, sandpaper,
Smooth wood, powdery chalk,
Water.

Where does it live?
It lives in - the best places on Earth,
Or the worst,
In everyone.

What does it smell like?
It smells like - roses, manure,
Ugly perfume, a baby's bum,
Snow.

What would it say if it could speak?
It would say - everything.

Megan Gracie (14)
Hawick High School, Hawick

The River's Journey To The Sea!

A
   Tiny
     Trickle
       Slowly starts
         Running faster
          Down the hill
        Bouncing off the
              Rocks
          And
        Stones
          Like a tennis ball
            Changing direction
          All
            The time
              Then getting deeper
               Always growing
             Never stopping
           Slowly flowing
         A thick, blue scarf
        Thrown over a green field
      A slithering, silver snake winding
       A path through the grass
         Curving round the trees
       But never touching them
      Wider now and almost black
     Metal cranes guarding the banks
     Tall soldiers guiding the river to the sea!

Rebecca Lee (13)
Hawick High School, Hawick

Moon

God turns the light off,
But leaves a candle burning.
The candle slowly dies,
As the world is turning.

Sunshine is off to bed,
He leaves his white dog out on the lawn,
Or maybe the sky is just afraid of the dark,
And needs a nightlight on.

A big panic button,
A precious jewel,
An empty plate,
A shimmering pool.

A patrol officer on duty,
Makes sure the kids are in bed,
A haunted torch
To provide light for the dead.

A spill of Tipp-Ex
As the sky does its essay.
A giant eye
Which shuts during the day.

A big birthday cake,
Sometimes half eaten.
A nightclub in the sky
Which aliens can meet in.

Mairi Cameron (13)
Hawick High School, Hawick

My Mum

My mum never stops cleaning,
She must be dreaming.

My mum never stops shouting,
She must be stressed.

My mum never stops cooking,
She must be bored.

My mum never stops chatting,
She must be tired.

My mum never stops working,
She must be desperate for a seat.

My mum never stops loving me,
She must be mad!

Mark Graham (14)
Hawick High School, Hawick

Snow Journey

Snow is the angels' tears falling from Heaven
Drifting gently, calmly onto the ground
Powder-white, winter blossom
A shining, white blanket of silk

Snow is a vast, frozen lake
Lying still and quiet
A shimmering field of diamonds
Hiding everything in sight

Snow is our childhood melting
Disappearing from view
Hear the trickle of running water
The wonderland has gone.

Ashley Drysdale (13)
Hawick High School, Hawick

The Sun Is . . .

A big, yellow beach ball in a huge swimming pool,
A bowl of steaming custard,
A fried egg with the white already eaten,
A jar of fiery mustard,

A butterball, a traffic light,
A microwave heating the land,
A yellow tomato, a light bulb,
A shiny pound coin in your hand.

And then before dusk
It starts to rust
Gives a warm tinge to the sky.
The orange glow reminds me of a fiery dragon's eye.

A ginger cat curled up, all snug,
By a fire of burning coals,
A pile of cornflakes, all crispy,
In a pinky orange bowl.

Sarah Thompson (13)
Hawick High School, Hawick

Anger

It would scream, 'Die!' if it could talk, or just howl.
It would live in Hell.
It's black.
It's red.
It would smell like an exploded firework.
It would kill you if it met you.
It would taste like stale blood.
It would feel sharp, like a blade of an axe.
It would feel like you'd explode.
Its friends are frustration, sadness and rage,
Although it doesn't get along with them.
Its favourite game is killing.

It's anger.

James McPherson (14)
Hawick High School, Hawick

What Is Happiness?

What is happiness?
Happiness looks like the sea on a tropical island.
It looks like the sky on a warm, summer's day.
It looks like my dad's face when Celtic are about to play.

What is happiness?
Happiness sounds like the birds singing early in the morning.
It sounds like people talking with their friends.
It sounds like my mum laughing when Ant and Dec ends.

What is happiness?
Happiness tastes like a big box of chocolates.
It tastes like a big glass of cold orange juice.
It tastes like my mum's chocolate mousse.

What is happiness?
Happiness feels like a warm hot water bottle.
It feels like a fluffy, sheepskin rug.
It feels like a long, loving hug.

What is happiness?
Happiness smells like a big bunch of flowers.
It smells like a big tub of sweet, sticky honey.
It smells like a great big bundle of money.

What is happiness?
If happiness could talk, it would say,
'Hip hip hooray,
Come out and play!'

What is happiness?
Happiness lives in your heart.
It lives with your family and friends.
It lives and lives and never ends.

Gillian Hogg (14)
Hawick High School, Hawick

Love

Love can *look* like two doves,
Gazing as if they had just met,
Looking deep into the other's eyes,
Flying wing on wing into the sunset.

Love can *sound* like a harp,
With its vibrant, rich strings,
Playing happily away to the world,
Contentedly thinking of other things.

Love can *taste* like butter,
Melting onto warm, soft toast,
The texture smooth in your mouth,
And reminding you of the heat of the coast.

Love can *feel* like clouds,
Floating wondrously amongst the many skies
With the views and space of the gods,
Never having to steal, cheat or lie.

Love can *live* in the depth of the sea,
Among the tropics and corals deep down,
Swimming amongst the fish and dolphins,
Smiling and laughing - never a frown.

Love can *smell* like chocolate,
A favourite to most of us,
Always loving and trying to please,
Rich, dark and mysterious.

Love can *say* many things,
Sweet, caring and kind,
But sometimes it just sits there,
Thinking and reading your mind.

Caitlin Hamilton (13)
Hawick High School, Hawick

The Sea

The darkness turned blue,
Dragged the boats to their dying depths,
Engulfed in those deep, dark waves,
The toll rises for seaman deaths.

The darkness turned blue,
The lighthouse stands tall,
As the current directs,
The boat towards the oncoming squall.

The darkness turned blue,
Relentless waves smash the boat like fists,
Holes punctured in the rotting, old wood,
Not a boat found land in the heart of the mists.

The darkness turned blue,
As the waves go slap, crack,
The boat gets plunged,
Into eternal black.

Greg Stark (13)
Hawick High School, Hawick

Snow

The snow is like a big, soft blanket,
A blanket that will always keep you warm.
Warm like you're snuggled up in your bed,
Your bed where you can relax.
Relax like you've not a care in the world,
The world where you always seem tiny.
Tiny like you don't even count,
Count to the people who are rich and famous.
Rich and famous people think they don't need to care,
Care like you should if you were normal.
Normal is different to every single person,
Every single person is very unique.
Unique is special; even if you don't think so.

Lois Niblo (13)
Hawick High School, Hawick

Boredom

Nowhere to go, nowhere to play
A football match, a rainy day.

A flat drink, a sugary tea
A coffee with milk just for me.

A hard rock, a thick wall
A bolted-down shed, a quiet market stall.

A scented candle, a cheap bathroom spray
Freebie perfume, unused hay.

A cardboard box, a black bag
A smelly old skip, underneath an old rag.

A ticking clock, a ringing phone
Bees buzzing, a toddler's moan.

'Let me out, give me some fun,'
That's what it would say if it could run.

Kieran Willison (13)
Hawick High School, Hawick

Nature

The wind howls as it rustles the leaves,
The leaves move along the concrete pavement,
The pavement directs them into a fence,
The fence collects them in a pile,
The pile scatters onto the long, green grass,
The long, green grass runs up to a hedge,
The hedge is surrounded on one side by gravel,
The gravel gets kicked into the plant bed,
The plant bed is home to plants and insects,
The insects live under the soil,
The soil soaks up all of the rain,
Some of the rain lands in the stream,
The water flows gently past the reeds,
The reeds sway in the wind,
The wind howls as it rustles the leaves.

Jak Scott (13)
Hawick High School, Hawick

Sadness

If you've ever been sad
You know how it feels.

Sadness would look like a lonely cow
In an empty, muddy field.

It would sound like the cry of a whale
Surrounded by gallons of water.

A single grape would taste of sadness
Sadness that went sour.

Sadness would feel like a powerful punch
From the biggest bully there ever was.

It would live in a dark cave
Up high on a mountain.

Sadness would smell of cooked fish
Fish that was old and smelly.

And sadness would say nothing at all
It would just cry.

Jaimie Nichol (14)
Hawick High School, Hawick

Loneliness

Loneliness is a dirty penny in the gutter waiting to be found,
Loneliness is starvation,
Loneliness is locked in a dark, cold, empty cupboard,
Loneliness the suffocating smell of wet in the car.
Loneliness is the sound of one word: silence.

Toni Pearce (12)
Hawick High School, Hawick

What Are Fairies?

What are fairies?
I really wonder what
Is it true about the tooth fairy,
Or should it be forgot?

Are they charming creatures,
Sweet, pretty and kind?
Are they adorable princesses,
Sickening the mind?

Do they wear long dresses,
Made from delicate leaves?
Do they use yellow flowers,
To make their golden sleeves?

Or are they ugly creatures,
All green, slimy and stink?
That is definitely not the sort,
The boys would like to wink.

Do they live in mud swamps,
Or black, sticky hollows?
Does the king pick his nose,
During the time he wallows?

Or are fairies myths,
Magical made-up lies?
Or are they in your garden,
Waiting to give you a surprise?

Emma Atkinson (12)
Inverness Royal Academy, Inverness

A Broken Heart

Today I sit alone with hurt in my heart
Needing to go on with my life
But not knowing where to start.

Why must I be alone and hurting in this painful way
When we were so happy?
Seems like only yesterday.

I really feel that my life has been wasted
Now there is nothing I can do
But spend what time I have left
Trying to get over you.

When we fell in love
I thought it would never end
Now I must try and find a way
For this broken heart to mend.

Although you're gone
You're forever in my heart
In my life you'll always be
The most important part.

Aysa Basbayraktar (13)
Inverness Royal Academy, Inverness

Getting Older

When I lay in my bed at night
I think what I will be like when I am older.
It would be great to be old. No school.
No homework. Just sit around each day.
But now I'm getting older I realise
It isn't as easy as that.
Pay bills. Pay tax. Pay mortgages.
So I think while I am young
Now I may as well enjoy it.

Gary James Paterson (13)
Inverness Royal Academy, Inverness

31st October

Pointed nose, crooked and cracked
A wart upon my chin
My long cloak came down past my knees
'Knock, knock!' called Kym.

We are off trick or treating
Collecting sweets and more
Away on our broomsticks
Going from door to door.

Telling our jokes
Or playing our tricks
Let's hope they give us some sweets
If not they will be in for a fix!

On our way home feeling cold and damp
We see the pumpkins glowing
Our witchy days are over again
And soon it will be snowing!

Lauren Cormack (13)
Inverness Royal Academy, Inverness

My Dog

My dog loves walks in the countryside,
With his head and tail high looking full of pride,
When we go to the beach he runs in the sand,
Swims in the sea and plays on the land.
He knows he's done wrong if I'm looking mad,
But how can I be when he's looking so sad?
He looks at me with his big, brown eyes,
Puts his head on my knee and whines and cries.
He's caring and loving, a fur ball of joy,
He is most happy when he gets a new toy.
He bathes in the sun and plays in the snow,
To me he's the best dog I'll ever know!

Mhairi Devlin (13)
Inverness Royal Academy, Inverness

The Blitz

I remember the Blitz like yesterday
I was lying in my bed
When suddenly I heard it -
The wailing of the siren
It rang in my ears
As we ran to the shelter.

The minutes passed like hours
I tried to get some sleep
But all I could think of was one thing -
My dad and grandpa out fighting.
After what seemed like days
The all-clear sounded
We thought it was all over
But then again
We never knew with Hitler
He'd probably strike again.

Hayley Scerri Davey (12)
Inverness Royal Academy, Inverness

A War Poem

There's bombs dropping,
And guns firing,
It should be stopping,
Everyone is crying.

Germans laughing,
Guns strafing,
Jews are dying,
Kids are crying.

Clothes are torn,
We should be warned,
We all have sworn,
That Hitler will be thorned.

Scott Melvin (12)
Inverness Royal Academy, Inverness

Mother Nature

When the wind blows,
Mother Nature blows you a kiss.
When it is raining,
Mother Nature is rinsing out the clouds.
When the fog rolls over the hills,
Mother Nature wants us to look after ourselves.

When there are stars in the sky,
Mother Nature is shining with joy.
When the sun is shining,
Mother Nature is glowing with happiness.
When the ice forms,
Mother Nature wants us to slow down and admire her beauty.

When there is thunder,
Mother Nature is in a bad mood.
When it snows,
Mother Nature wants us in awe of her power.

Natalie Craib (12)
Inverness Royal Academy, Inverness

Darkness

Your mum tucks you in and kisses you goodnight
Then shuts the door and switches off the light.
From having your mum at your side feeling safe and secure
You're now surrounded in darkness and now not so sure.
The shadows from the window are creating scary shapes
Of monsters, ghouls and ghosts, and scary men in capes.
You shiver under the blanket just hoping they disappear
But the darkness closes in and their noise you can hear.
You're shaking, frightened, terrified and let out a terrible scream
To find yourself in your mother's arms saying,
'There, there, it's only a dream.'

Carlena Kenley (12)
Inverness Royal Academy, Inverness

War

Guns, guns everywhere.
Bombs dropping on your house.
Babies screaming.
All started because of a mouse.

Hiding behind his Nazi army.
A little coward!
Executing innocent Jews.
The poor guy's name was Howard.

Bombers and fighters in the air -
Shooting each other down.
Germans fighting unfairly and
The war is against us now.

We paratroop into France
On the sixth of June.
All the soldiers are now saying:
'Hitler, you're going doon!'

We're beside that city now,
Getting close to him.
Their morale is dropping.
Their flame of evil
Is now starting to dim.

John MacLean (12)
Inverness Royal Academy, Inverness

My Pet

My pet stares up at me,
Begging and pleading for attention,
Or a hug or maybe a simple compliment
Or smile towards him.

I stare back at him and see
His misery for receiving none
Of these. I lean down and say
His name and give him a pat.

Instantly joy floods into his
Eyes and his tail starts to wag.
I give him a big hug and a
Treat. For now, he is content.

But he will not always be
Content and happy. At some
Point his joy will cease. It may
Be for a second, minute or hour.

Only one thing is certain,
That when I see my pet once
More and give him my love, his tail
Will begin to move, then wag again.

He will be content
Once more.

Hannah Burgess (13)
Inverness Royal Academy, Inverness

Summer!

Summer fun
In the sun

Water fights
Long, hot nights

Time to play
Hip hip hooray

Ice lollies, icy cool
It's time to play in the pool

Sandcastles on the beach
Whosever is the biggest gets a peach

Barbecues, oh what fun
Mine's a burger in a bun

Someone's got a trampoline
Come and bounce, we're full of beans

Someone suggests butterflies as pets
Wouldn't you like one in your net?

Picnic baskets at the ready
Don't forget to bring your teddy

Splashing in the paddling pool
Don't I look like such a fool?

Rebecca L Black (13)
Inverness Royal Academy, Inverness

A World Without Words

Could you say *'I can live without words'*
As if words don't even matter?
Believe it or not you are actually saying
'I can live without reading'
'I can live without writing'
'I can live without talking'
'I can even live without thinking'
Can you imagine the chaos
If there was suddenly no language,
No ways or means of communication
To whisper the name you called your own?
The world starts over again
Your wonderful ideas disappeared
But it wouldn't matter anyway
You wouldn't be able to talk
So next time someone asks you
'Could you live without words?'
Just remember this
The world can't live without words
I can't
Can you?

Lindsey Stirling (13)
Inverness Royal Academy, Inverness

The Clydebank Blitz

The house shakes
I sit up in bed
People are screaming
Echoes run through my head.

I run down the stairs
Out the back door
I get to the shelter
And sit on the floor.

Incendiaries fall
They light up the city
Houses fall down
Oh what a pity.

At last the all-clear
Nervously I look all around
Is my house there?
No - it has crashed to the ground.

Helen Duncan (12)
Inverness Royal Academy, Inverness

Death

Death is the end of the road,
The thing which comes for everyone,
And it never misses,
Never.

Once it happens,
There is no turning back,
Death will take you from everything you know,
And leave you in a place of which
No one knows.

For some it is sudden,
Some it is a welcomed gift,
But one thing is for sure,
Death is swift.

John Fraser (13)
Inverness Royal Academy, Inverness

Morning

It's morning.
Time to get up
And get ready for school.

I hear the creaking of the lock.
The banging of the door.
The sound of people yakking,
While getting out of bed.

The sound of pouring milk,
Splashing into the bowl.
The sound of people crunching,
While getting ready for school.

The sound of whistling birds.
The quacking of the ducks.
The sound of the whispering wind,
While walking to school.

Anna Ferguson (13)
Inverness Royal Academy, Inverness

This Morning

This morning I didn't want to lift my head
I didn't even want to get out of bed

This morning I didn't want to take a shower
I just wanted to listen to the clock tick away another hour

This morning I didn't want to eat breakfast
I tried to make it go away but I just made the hunger last

This morning I didn't want to get dressed
I just wanted a couple more minutes' rest

This morning I didn't want to go out the door
I didn't want to be awake anymore

This morning I watched a bird glide
This morning I put on my coat and went outside.

Rachael Morrison (12)
Inverness Royal Academy, Inverness

Our World

Animals, insects
Mammals or man
We roam the Earth
Looking quite calm

Water, wind
Sun and rain
Without these
We would go insane

Moon and stars
Dark skies at night
To see the planets
An amazing sight

Flowers and trees
And under the sea
Plant life and fish
Birds and the bees

Toddlers, teenagers
Adults and 'oldies'
Different ages
Different nationalities

War and peace
Wealth and famine
Our Earth is scarred
By so many grabbin'

Our world is full
Of wonderful things
But best of all
Comes family and friends.

Adele MacPherson (12)
Inverness Royal Academy, Inverness

Holidays!

Holidays are really great,
And I think you are bound,
To look forward to holidays,
All year round.

Holidays are away from home,
Having loads of fun,
Holidays are not rain or clouds,
But lots and lots of sun.

On holiday you can make new pals,
And play with them a lot,
It's rarely cold on holiday,
But very, very hot.

Swimming pool every day,
And eating ice creams,
And in some countries you have a nap,
While dreaming loads of dreams.

Along with all the swimming pools,
You can also go to the beach,
And best of all no more school,
For all the teachers to teach.

Going out for tea,
Staying up late at nights,
Travelling around,
Seeing all the famous sights.

But soon the time will come,
To say goodbye,
And off you go back home,
With a big, long sigh.

Kelly Goddard (13)
Inverness Royal Academy, Inverness

The Pewits

Under the after-sunset sky
Two pewits sport and cry
But white the fox is, low and sly
He does not like the pewits' cry

So low he lies among the grass
No small detail does he surpass
The birds fly low, the fox does see
So he jumps up and catches thee

And now the tragic tale unfolds
With one bird gone, the other low
The fox not full, jumps up again
Now they are gone, not seen again

Alas, now no two pewits fly
Soaring up in the springtime sky
So the tale does sadly end
The little pewits are both at an end.

Alexander Mount (13)
Inverness Royal Academy, Inverness

Death

Death,
Is what you want it to be,
Darkness is darkness,
It may happen to you soon,
And by then you will be lifeless.

Sadness is a tear from your eye,
A dream may be what you think,
But then,
It's actually a time to say goodbye.

It's like a never-ending, darkened room,
No colour, no sound,
But in five minutes,
You will end up under the ground.

Brendan To (13)
Inverness Royal Academy, Inverness

Suicide Of A Broken Heart

His hands clicking
His eyes flicking

He sits in the corner
A broken-hearted mourner

When in his heart
As if pierced by a dart

Love's lost glare
Inflames his despair

As he cries on the floor
He reaches for the drawer

As his thumb feels its run
Down the satin of the gun

Racked with love's pains
He blows out his brains.

Rhian T Starkey (13)
Inverness Royal Academy, Inverness

Privilege Of Youth?

H ippy hairstyles,
A rranged in red and blue,
I ndigo the colour for me and you,
R eplicating fashions of the celebrity world

A nother hippy in my glare,
N utty styles your view to treat,
D andelions just simply can't compete

B ushy eyebrows we have to rid,
E nsuring eyes that are so hip,
A nguish of a teenage life,
U nblemished images to protect,
T aunting jeers to avoid,
Y outh, desirable or not?

Desre Stewart (12)
Inverness Royal Academy, Inverness

Forgotten

I lie here in the earth
My gravestone bears no name
Who was I? No one knows
There are many more the same
One dying tree marks my rest
Nothing else remains
Who was I? No one knows
There are many more the same
Dead flowers and dried tears
No body and no name
Who was I? No one knows
There are many more the same
I am the forgotten one
The one without a name
Who was I? No one knows
There are many more the same.

Iona Rule (13)
Inverness Royal Academy, Inverness

Death

Death is dark, death is evil
Death is a never-ending
Darkened room
Death is a tunnel of evil
Little creatures coming
To take away your spirit forever
Death is worse than your worst nightmare
Death is what you make it.

Enjoy!

Martin Munro (14)
Inverness Royal Academy, Inverness

Cat Food

There it goes.
That wild cat.
Right off the couch
And at that rat.

She flies right at it.
Across the room.
Mouse better run
Or meet its doom.

Mouse drops its snack.
Runs for cover.
But it's too late . . .
Cat grabs that rat.

She picks it up.
She lets it run.
She grabs it again
Just for fun.

She grabs the mouse
And throws it about.
One last chomp.
Poor mouse is gone.

Off it goes.
That wild cat.
Back on the couch
To snooze again.

Finlay Sutherland (13)
Inverness Royal Academy, Inverness

Windsurfing

Out on Loch Ness
Surfing my best
The sun shining down
With my dad like a clown

He jumps up and down
Trying to get brown
Prancing around
Oh! what a clown

Feeling the cold in-between my toes
My stomach knots like a garden hose
Holding the mast
Going like a blast
The wind blowing fast
I hope this will last

Watching the sun set
Surfing back in
What a fab day
I wish I could stay
Out on Loch Ness
Surfing my best.

Karen Innes (12)
Inverness Royal Academy, Inverness

What Is Death?

Death is what you want it to be,
It is a darkened room,
Inside your heart.
Eternal! Eternal!

Sadness is the world of death,
It's a tear in your eye,
Darkness is darkness,
Death is death.

Death will strike at any time.
It looms in the darkness,
And moves away from the light.
Eternal damnation!

So what is death?
It is where you can't break free,
Where you are destined for doom?
Where you're walking down that long, dark road,
That is death!

Becky Donaldson (14)
Inverness Royal Academy, Inverness

The Cult Of The Supreme Being

The Cult of the Supreme Being
Was empowered with divine commission.
While I raised my head, down in the stocks,
Submitting to my superstition.
Heaven sent me lethargy and a pen,
Twice caught down with all my class.
Coughing up blood, and eight a day,
I broke the dreams she made with glass.

Storming the Bastille with word from the king,
Danton and me make society.
And oh my God, give me strength, just don't give me company.
Oh tonight's a beautiful night, oh tonight, there's no need to fight.
But I feel I'm losing sight of my dreams, or so it seems.

Those who don't fear death never die, and I'll never die.

Static as I am, I'm just more delicate, calculating my reproach.
But with this heart, that grows and groans,
Stealing the love, as I approach.

And I'm so confused, but it seems to keep you amused,
But I feel I'm being used when you tell me I'm nothing new.
Oh tonight's a beautiful night, oh tonight, there's no need to fight.
But I feel I'm losing sight of my dreams, or so it seems.

Life's just a waste of time, and art's just a frame of mind.
So The Cult of the Supreme Being
Was empowered with divine commission.

Sam James Mitchell Hayward (16)
Lancaster Royal Grammar School, Lancaster

Selfish

He had been so cruel,
So careless,
So selfish.

Took to the wheel,
Without haste,
Without thought.

Intoxicated by society's demoralising liquor,
Without haste,
Without thought.

And now, I lie here, surrounded by red pain,
Warm, yet cold.
I'd only been out with friends,
I had done no wrong,
Why? Why had he done this?
Without haste,
Without thought.

Everyone hovers above my broken body,
Trying to help,
But they can't,
They can't go back and stop him,
Being,
So careless,
So selfish.

Without haste,
Without thought.

Still, I lay here, in decay,
Physical decay,
Mental decay,
Poetic decay . . .

Andy Cooper (14)
Lancaster Royal Grammar School, Lancaster

Dragon School

I set off up the sleeping dragon's back,
Right the way up its vertebrae, traffic light hump,
Lying underground waiting for me to arrive on time in its belly,
Rules - 'to the left', 'no eating', 'no pushing' keeps me in order,
Commuters - the dreaded machines turning us into druids
Ready to be hypnotised into the open, waiting jaws.

Wet lunch breaks, huddle up in shelter,
Like ducklings under their mother,
Science lessons - a recipe book for the whole world,
With ingredients, methods and plans.
Words, paragraphs, apostrophes, translation, reading,
Textbooks with the smell of the past, tell of the past present.
We dream of the future.

Games - freedom - we race and chase, wild ponies,
Let loose from our chains.
We can see the dragon's crown upon its head waiting for us.

Jacob Jolleys (15)
Lancaster Royal Grammar School, Lancaster

You Remember Me?

Do you remember me when the moon is high?
When the wind is east or when the clouds are blue?
In the morning mist, in the daytime breeze,
Or when the sun has risen?
If the trees are bare and the streets are clear
Will you remember me?

If the days are slow and the time is 12,
Will you remember me?
Or if the birds do sing and the water shines in the sunshine,
Will you remember me?
I can see the stars, I can see the diamond mountains,
I can't see nothing but still,
Will you remember me?

Jamie Pedrick (16)
Oriel High School, Great Yarmouth

Guardian Angel

You were always there in my time of need,
You had the plaster when I did bleed.
You had the shoulder when I did cry,
Why is it you had to die?
I thought we'd be forever apart,
I thought no one could mend my bleeding heart.
Until the day I got the sign of love,
From that guardian angel of mine.
That guardian angel which I now confide everything to.
That guardian angel, it turns out,
Happens to be you.

Christina Stranks (13)
Oriel High School, Great Yarmouth

Elderly Deceiver

That elderly deceiver,
Told me she was a weaver,
And that elderly deceiver,
Got me to believe her.

Spotted her in blue,
Uniform it was too!
Driving past the zoo,
And in public too.

Investigate was what I did,
Who would notice one small kid?
Behind a tree was where I hid,
Who would notice one small kid?

She really drived a great big bus,
And never liked to make a fuss.
Because she was an old deceiver,
She never really was a weaver.

Meghan Hook Mackey (13)
Ross High School, Tranent

The Uses Of A Walking Stick

A walking stick is a useful thing,
Especially for hitting fences - *ding, ding, ding.*
It is also good for a huge number of reasons,
Especially to pinpoint the seasons.
In winter the stick freezes over.
In spring it is covered in clover.
In summer it is too hot to handle.
In autumn it gets so dark I need a candle.
A way in which it can be used is to defend you,
As when you are bothered by a troubled youth.
Then you hit them with all your might,
Then they run until it stops being light.
And finally it is good for walking,
Or to stop someone talking.

Jack Manus (14)
Ross High School, Tranent

Walking Sticks

Walking sticks are useful things,
With the help they give people.
But elderly people hit us 'whippersnappers' with it!
They take advantage of a useful stick,
Half of them can walk on their own.
With their 'so-called' fragile bones,
They are just a bunch of old moans.
In my day, blah, blah, blah,
Never at school long enough.
Thinking they are respected and bold,
I think they just smell of old mould.
I don't like old people.

Daryl Manson (14)
Ross High School, Tranent

A Man's Best Friend

Mr Black shuffled slowly down the street,
Really he has no beat

Caring for his wife all night and day
Has made him look rather grey

Really if it wasn't for his wife May
He would be ever so lonely day after day

Unfortunately Mrs Black died
Mr Black cried and cried

A few weeks later Molly appeared
She was a collie dog who was lost and lonely

Now Mr Black isn't so alone
Molly is by his side with a very tasty bone.

Claire Bowie (13)
Ross High School, Tranent

Because I Am Old

When I am old I'll climb a tree,
Then I will fall and bash my knee.
I'll learn to spit,
And try to knot.
I'll get a mention,
When I get my pension.
I'll get a new hat,
And steal people's cats.
I'll eat sweets,
And sleep on the streets.
I'll write a will,
And send people my bill.
I'll run a marathon in the cold,
And I'll do all this because I am old.

Lauren Ritchie
Ross High School, Tranent

When I Am Old

When I am old,
I'll get wrinkly and cold,
Go down hills in a wheelchair,
Like a speeding bull,
Dodging around people,
Racing other old men,
At the bottom I'll crash into a tree,
Fall off my wheelchair and bang my knee.

Trip people up with my walking stick,
Sitting on the park bench with my good old friend Dick,
People fall flat on their face,
When they get up they'll have a look of disgrace.

At night sneak out with scissors,
Into the neighbour's garden,
And *snip, snip, snip,* off with their heads,
Flower heads lying in a heap,
In the morning they would go berserk,
But wouldn't blame an old man like me.

Walk into a supermarket with a big bag,
Leaving my scooter at the exit,
Steal cans of food from the shelves,
Walk out the exit with the alarms going off,
Jump on my scooter and drive away.

And finally scare the young children,
With my false teeth chasing after them,
Crying to their mums but I'd be off,
No one would suspect an old man like me!

Daniel Graham (14)
Ross High School, Tranent

Imagine . . .

When I am old I will tell stories of my youth,
And slide down the banister and chip a tooth!
I will go to the dentist to obtain false teeth,
And they will be as shiny as an aluminium sheath!

I will watch slithery snakes that crawl through the grass,
And score a goal at the football match!
I will jump off a trampoline high in the sky,
And when no one is expecting me to I'll scream, *'I can fly!'*

When I am old I will wear silly hats,
And skirts mixed red and black,
I will stroll into a youth clothes shop,
And when I can't find the right size
They'll wonder why I have lost the plot!

I will guzzle my guts full of chocolate and crisps,
And when I gain the weight who cares if I look the pits!
I will go for a run with tiny shorts on,
And sit in the middle of the path when all my energy's gone!

When I am old I will sneak out at night,
And set the neighbour's garden alight,
But before I do I will collect all the pretty shrubs,
And set them on my window in a large tub!

I will sit in a wheelchair at the top of a hill,
No one will think I'll roll down but I will!
I will zoom and swoosh and glide and dodge,
And make sure I finish first at the granny lodge!

Danielle Henderson (14)
Ross High School, Tranent

Is This Granny Wacky?

Off she goes to the bathroom with her shower cap on,
Pops her teeth in, *clack, clack, clack.*
She toddles downstairs,
Has her Weetabix, *chomp, chomp, chomp.*

There she goes shuffling down the street,
Talking to everyone she meets.
Wearing her wacky, brightly-coloured clothes,
Looking like a clown!

On the park bench she sits,
Acting quite normal,
Then suddenly she springs out at people,
And they run away.

At night she plays chap door run,
Then hides behind trees and has fun!
She goes to bed laughing her head off,
Thinking she is great!

The next day she starts again,
Isn't she a wacky granny?

Gillian McGlashan (13)
Ross High School, Tranent

When I Am Old

When I am old I'll buy hundreds of dogs,
They will be smarter than humans and jump over logs.
I'll shoot people from my window with a BB gun,
Then after I'll go and have a cream bun.
I'll eat lots of sweets,
And go running down the streets.
I'll hit people with my walking stick,
Then I'll show them a funny trick.
I'll move to Brazil,
But I will not take my pill.
I will get a tan,
Then drink from a cola can.
I will be shrivelled as a prune,
I'll never use a spoon.
I will steal a policeman's hat,
And run over cats.
I'll get drunk every night,
Then get in a fight.
This is what I'll do when I'm old,
And I start to grow mould.

Max Newcombe
Ross High School, Tranent

Old But Young

When you are old you can still be young,
Climbing trees just for fun.
Scaring pigeons off a seat,
Chasing people down the street.
Race your scooter down a hill,
Steal all the money from the till.
Hit people with your stick,
Walk by and give them a kick.
Squeal, scream, shout and pout,
Jump up and down when you're out.
Cause a riot in the shops,
Get a chase from the cops.
Play football in the street,
Knock people off their feet.
Steal the neighbour's flowers at night,
Put them on the window sill in plain sight.
Moan about your son's behaviour,
Then go out skating an hour later.
So when you're old remember to be young at heart,
Wild and free.

Stephanie Armstrong
Ross High School, Tranent

A Typical Grandad Who Was Special

My grandad was typical.
He would moan when rap music was played,
He would use a walking stick,
But not a wheelchair,
He could walk for miles before his puffer was used,
He was like Superman,
That's what made him special.

My grandad was typical.
He would wear the oddest clothes,
He would wear a bonnet,
But not a baseball cap,
He could teach anyone to fish,
He could have been the greatest fisherman ever,
That's what made him special.

My grandad was typical.
He would read the paper for hours,
He would drink tea,
But not coffee,
He could grow the best vegetables,
That's what made him special.

Raymond Hill (13)
Ross High School, Tranent

When I Grow Old

When I grow old I'll smoke a fag
And wear my clothes inside out,
I'll make sure I have some fun
When I grow old.

I'll wear a bright orange jacket
Like a ball of fire
And embarrass everyone who knows me.
Then I'll hit all the children with my walking stick
To make them cry
When I grow old.

And when I get in trouble I'll pie the police
And get chased down the street in my mobile buggy.
Then I'll go home and act normally so no one knows.
Then *bang* I'm at it again
When I grow old.

So when it's my time to go,
Everyone will miss me.
I'll scream in Heaven,
I'll scream in Hell.
Yes, when I grow old.

Jennifer Kerr (13)
Ross High School, Tranent

When I'm Old

When I'm old I'll be happy as ever,
My family will think never,
Is that my granny running down,
Down that street and round the town?
That's not all I'll do,
I will make them take me to the loo,
Wipe my bum when they say there's nothing to do.
When I'm old I'll hit all the children that I don't like,
Especially that little boy Mike,
He's always in my way on his bike,
Him and his friends think they are cool,
I'll show them when I throw them in the pool.
I'd like to steal some sweets from a shop,
Burst a bag in someone's ear, *pop!*
Everyone will scream in horror.
Smash a window and blame it on the kids.
I will throw dogs' poo at all the windows.
I would love to hit a police officer with a bat,
Or run around after a cat.
These are the things I will do when I'm old.
Do you think you will do them too?

Kirsty Stewart
Ross High School, Tranent

When I Am Old . . .

When I am old . . .
I'll hit people with my electric scooter,
And annoy my grandson's tutor.
I'll never run out of my wonderful luck,
And when I get to the park I'll strangle a duck.

When I was young . . .
I couldn't drive a car insanely,
I now do it for fun mainly.
I couldn't smack my grandson,
Now I do it for fun.

When I am shopping . . .
I run in and steal food,
And am known to be hard and that's not good.
I grab the money from the till,
And grab the scooter and zoom down the hill.
I've set the record for the longest police chase,
And the look on the guy behind's face!
I've set the record for the longest police chase
Of one hundred and forty-one cars,
But when they caught me they put me behind bars.
I thought, *is this my fate,*
To be boxed into a crate?

Jamie Balfour (13)
Ross High School, Tranent

Bad Granny

There's a really bad granny somewhere in the world,
Who throws snotty bogies at young children,
And if she is walking with her walking stick,
If there's anyone in sight,
She hits them with her stick,
Like bullets coming out of a gun!

There's a really bad granny somewhere in the world,
Whose breath smells like a pig's den,
And spits non-stop,
Like a forever-running tap!
And once a young child,
Even mistook her nose,
To be a dirty, brown branch.

There's a really bad granny somewhere in the world,
Who wears bright, fluorescent pink skirts,
And fake tan,
As bright as the sun!
She wears a wig which looks like a sheep.
And owns a dog that sounds
Like a broken foghorn!

There's a really bad granny somewhere in the world,
Who lives in a mind, in the middle of an imagination.
That really bad granny lives . . .
In my mind!

Amanda Veal
Ross High School, Tranent

What I'd Like To Do When I'm Old!

When I'm old I'd like to
Go down a hill in my wheelchair,
Swerve in and out of people,
Knock them over,
Watch them roll down the hill beside you,
Put my hand in people's handbags,
Steal purses and valuables.

I would like to stand at my gate,
Wait for school children to walk past,
And hit them hard so they would run home.
They would be screaming so loud,
It would be like a lion roaring.
When they go in they would have a bright red . . .?

I would love to go about in my electric scooter,
And go past houses and hit windows with smelly eggs,
Which go *splat!*
I would throw them at people who weren't watching,
That would teach them a lesson for not watching!

Daniel McNeill
Ross High School, Tranent

Ending

The money that we once used to share,
Now is split in two, but I don't care.
The house I used to try to decorate and fail,
Now is abandoned and is up for sale.
The love that we used to call 'our own',
Now is locked away and all alone.
The teddy I bought you last year,
Now is deserted, full of fear.
The people who held hands side by side,
Are now confessing, their love has died.

Thomas Slapp (12)
Rushcliffe School, Nottingham

Glad I Am

I am:
The garden that is tended with bright blossoms
And exotic and perfumed flowers

I am:
The teddy bear that is hugged all day and night

I am:
The book that turns chapters every blink of an eye

I am:
The party that's full of laughter and joyful, happy, smiling people

I am:
The bright, brand new, shiny sports car that you dream of
Day in, day out

I am:
The golden mansion with butlers and maids
That do everything for you

I am your son.

Gurjeet Roth (13)
Rushcliffe School, Nottingham

Who Knows?

Soaring through the moonlight sky
Flying up and up so very high
Gently gliding on the breeze
The cold wind whistling through the trees
The sea lies so calm and still
The whole world sleeps until
The morning comes, the birds come out to sing
Who knows what the day will bring?

Daniel Sutherland (13)
Rushcliffe School, Nottingham

Let Me Be Your . . .

Let me be your blanket to sleep your day away,
Let me be your credit card to have some fun and play.
Let me be your shower to wash away your fears,
Let me be your teddy bear to wipe away your tears.

Let me be your shoes to walk you on the path of life,
Let me be your door to protect you from a knife.
Let me be your eyes to show you the way to go,
Let me be your boxing gloves to fight away a foe.

Let me be your glamorous car to drive away and play,
Let me be your light bulb to brighten up your day.
Let me be your raincoat to protect you from the rain,
Let me be your sticky leg wax, I won't give you any pain.

Let me be your hot chocolate to give you the perfect taste,
Let me be your perfect man, I won't be on your case.
Let me be your aeroplane to fly you to an exotic location,
Let me be your train ticket to take you to your destination.

Antonio Barlow (13)
Rushcliffe School, Nottingham

Your Love

Your love is like a fresh flower in spring
You make me feel a powerful king.
Your hair is as smooth as a hidden pearl
I want to look for it all over this world.
Your lips are as red as a red rose petal
It makes me feel like a shiny, new metal.
Your eyes are like a golden sun
I want to see them 24/7.
Your comforting breath I just love to hear
I want to be with you, always near.
Your gentle voice is like trickling water
But my patience for you is getting shorter.
You make me feel special and warm inside
But you left me alone, that day you lied.

Felicity Cooper (12)
Rushcliffe School, Nottingham

The End

The lips that were as red as cherries
Looked like they tasted of strawberries
They then spoke words of hatred and vengeance
Our loved passion is beyond amendance
The face that was as white as snow
Could not help feelings show
This face is now pinched and bitter
Covered in scowls of old litter
I stared into your deep blue eyes
It was in these where Heaven lies
They now lie dull, empty and listless
Looking like they have a death wish list
The hair that lay smooth and silky
The colour of Horlicks milky
This hair is now scraped back and is greased in stress
And I must say it looked a complete mess
The heart that spelt out pure passion
Has now silenced like it's fashion
The heart that would always beat like a clock
Now sits empty as it's come to a stop.

Harley Greener (12)
Rushcliffe School, Nottingham

Ending

The love that was once as deep as the ocean
Has turned to the waves, dragged from the shore in fast motion

The voices that sang like a morning in spring
Are the shrieks of an angel with only one wing

The hearts that would once open wide like a door
Are sealed shut so no one can explore

The smiles that would once brighten up each rainy day
Are smiles hiding tears, there is nothing left to say
Other than our love has gone away.

Ellen Malone (13)
Rushcliffe School, Nottingham

Sad I Ams

I am:

    The ice
    That sticks to your car
    The rain cloud
    That haunts you from afar
    The broken car
    I don't take you very far

I am:

    The lumpy bed
    On which you can't sleep
    The wolf
    Which eats all the sheep
    The onion
    That makes you weep

I am:

    The match
    That doesn't make a spark
    The monster
    That hides in the dark
    The stain
    That leaves a mark.

Flossie Eyden (13)
Rushcliffe School, Nottingham

My Love For You

Your bright blue eyes shine brighter than the stars
Your skin is more radiant than flowers
Because my love for you is taller than towers.

Your smile is as beautiful as flowers
It blows me away in the ghostly breeze
You stand there making everlasting poses
When we hold you fill me with ease.

My love for you is wider than oceans
When I'm with you I'm in a swirling motion.

Jade Cito (12)
Rushcliffe School, Nottingham

I Wanna Be Yours

(Based on 'I Wanna Be Yours' by John Cooper Clarke)

Let me be your hair curlers
To keep a spring in your step
Let me be your tissues
To wipe away the tears you've wept

Let me be your toothbrush
To refresh your life
Let me be your washing machine
To wash away your strife

    I wanna be yours

Let me be your table lamp
To help you through the mist
Let me be your mirror
To see the face I want to kiss

Let me be your photo frame
To keep our memories forever
Let me be your clock
So we can count time together

    I wanna be yours

Let me be your dictionary
I'll never be lost for words
Let me be your staircase
So we can fly as high as birds

Let me be your umbrella
I'll protect you from the wind and rain
Let me be your dishwasher
I'll take away your strain

    I wanna be yours.

Holly Wain (13)
Rushcliffe School, Nottingham

Ending

The smile that was once so warm and loving,
now scowls without hesitation.

The phone that was forever calling,
now a silent grave, not known to mourning.

Doors once invitingly ajar,
are now enclosed to secrets so far.

The promises that were kept for life,
now in tatters by a sharp, cruel knife.

The trust that shone deep in your eyes,
now gone and replaced with small, sad cries.

The smell of your innocent musk,
is now a scent of selfish lust.

Without a hope of finding amend
this relationship will have to end.

Vicki Clark (12)
Rushcliffe School, Nottingham

Untitled

A lonely flower which has survived many winds
A spider which collapsed in a bin
Is as sad as someone being sinned
My love is trapped in a solid gold tin

Our love is as tall as the London Tower
You look like a tulip in bloom
You make me feel red and sour
In your heart you must make room

Your eyes burn like the shiny moon
You shield me from despair and doubt
I love you lots, I'm coming pretty soon
To fix your broken water spout.

Sam Price (12)
Rushcliffe School, Nottingham

Ending

Our love was once a searing flame
Now it's burnt out and full of shame
Our love was like a magnificent tower
Now it's just a withered flower
I was once your loveable teddy
Now without you my life is bare
I just hang my head in despair.

Our once shared smiles thrown upside down
Now I carry a disgusting frown
The lips once red and always kissing
Now blue and desperately missing
Awakened by love but also destroyed
It just makes me really annoyed.

Alistair Britton (12)
Rushcliffe School, Nottingham

Let Me Be Your . . .

(Inspired by 'I Wanna Be Yours' by John Cooper Clarke)

Let me be your central heating, I will never fail
Let me be your umbrella, to protect you from the hail
Let me be your lock and key, to keep your life secure
Let me be your money bank, to make sure you're never poor

Let me be your television, to pass away the time
Let me be your dusting cloth, to clean away the grime
Let me be your light bulb, to brighten up your day
Let me be your board games, that you always want to play

Let me be your raffle tickets, I will always win
Let me be your Bible, to make sure you never sin
Let me be your plaster, to protect you from sores
I will do anything to be yours.

Dominic Lowes (13)
Rushcliffe School, Nottingham

Sad I Ams

I am:

> The excess oil
> That got washed up in the bay,
> The empty crisp packet
> Floating along the way,
> The rain
> On your wedding day.

I am:

> The battered book
> In a car boot sale,
> The black cloud
> That promises hail,
> The test paper
> That reads out *fail!*

I am:

> The smashed light bulb
> That no longer gives out light,
> The weeds in your garden
> That you wish were out of sight,
> In your nightmares
> That always give you a fright.

Paige Wilson (12)
Rushcliffe School, Nottingham

The Poor Old Dog

The old dog dozes on her faded, kitchen mat.
That's all she ever does these days.
Her body wrecked with arthritis.

She never used to be like this.
She used to be energetic and playful.
Now she only sleeps and eats and dreams.

Her owners pour some biscuits into her metal bowl.
The pinging noise awakes her.
She stirs and struggles to get up . . .

. . . Collapses,
Back legs trembling,
She whimpers in pain.

Brown eyes forlorn and pleading.

No more can she put pressure on her back legs.
No more walks,
Along the Lough shore.

Her owners stroke her head and encourage her.
'What's the humane thing to do?'
They ask.

Next week they take her to the vet's.
They shed their tears,
And bid farewell.

The old mat is empty now,
The pain that was is gone.
But sadness and fond memories,
Cast shadows on the floor.

Alan Barr (14)
St Louis Grammar School, Ballymena

As Free As A Bird

Up in the sky
The birds play up high
They open their beak
But they do not speak
Instead they play a tune
And each note is neither too late nor too soon
They play and they sing
Happiness is what they bring
And at night when they've finished their play
They find a warm place to sleep
Waiting for the next new day
They never speak a word
Because they're happy
As free as a bird.

Emma Dooey (12)
St Louis Grammar School, Ballymena

The Weird Things In My Head

The weird things in my head,
Keep swirling around and around,
Like how am I going to die,
Get shot and be lying on the ground?

I avoid the cracks in the pavement,
To see when Mum will be back,
I never see her now,
It's the only thing I lack.

The weird things in my head,
Just won't go away,
I want my mum back,
And I want her back to stay.

Shona O'Rawe (14)
St Louis Grammar School, Ballymena

Student

I always ask stupid questions
My teacher cannot stand me
I am a menace to my school
Someone should have banned me.

Whenever I stand up I am told to sit back down
Every time I speak the teacher has a frown.
When I go to school, I dread it every day
When I look at the teacher's face
It gets more evil in every way!

Christopher Docherty (13)
St Luke's High School, Barrhead

Poem

Motorbikes are fast
Motorbikes are fun
Motorbikes are loud
Fast over the jump
Slow over the jump
The thrill you get from riding one
You might fall off but that's fun
Motocross racing is fun.

Peter McAllister (12)
St Luke's High School, Barrhead

The Sun

The sun is blazing hot,
The sun is splitting the sky.
The sun is golden yellow,
The sun is hurting my eye.
The sun is sizzling,
Like a frying pan.

Fern Maxwell (12)
St Luke's High School, Barrhead

Poem On Bullying

Bullying is bad,
It makes me sad,
To see others hurt,
It makes me mad.

That horrible bully that bullies my friend,
Sticks around on that bend.

I think about it every night,
Every night I get a fright,
If I go cold,
What does my future hold?

I can't go on,
Is this all I am scared from?

Laura McDonald (12)
St Luke's High School, Barrhead

Friends

Friends! Friends! Friends!
They share make-up,
Fall out, then break up.
Friends! Friends!
What are they like?
It was only last week they went out on their bike!
Friends they care, love and share
With each other.
Just as if they were with their mother.
Girls now wear loads of pink to make the boys wink!

Megan McBride (12)
St Luke's High School, Barrhead

Foxes

If foxes came in boxes
And the boxes were all brown,
Then there might just be enough brown boxes
To give to the whole town.

But foxes are not brown,
So why have brown boxes to give to the whole town?
Why not have red?
Everyone likes red.

So there you are lying in your bed
And a little, red box is lying at your door.
The doorbell rings, the dog sings
And you open your door.

You lift it up, flip the lid
And see a little, red fox in a little, red box.
You drop it on the floor and run out the door.
There goes that little, red fox in that little, red box!

Martyn Wilson (13)
St Luke's High School, Barrhead

I'm Sitting In My Living Room

I'm sitting in my living room so bored I want to cry,
I'm sitting in my window staring into the sky,
I look at the time, oh it's only half-past nine,
There's nothing on the TV, oh what can I do?
I'm going to go to bed now
As I'm so bored I want to cry!

Kayleigh McPherson (13)
St Luke's High School, Barrhead

Locked Away

As I look out of the window,
The rain falls from the sky.
I can hear the sound of
Children's laughter far away.

I wish I were back home,
Sitting by the fire.
Why did they have to believe that liar?
It's her fault I am here.

I look past the steel bars
Of my tiny cell room.
All I can see is
Blank, white doors.

I can hear the clanking of
Doors, people getting out.
I don't care because
This place is unfair.

Jane Lunday (13)
St Luke's High School, Barrhead

Barney

B arney is my cat
A black and white one too
R eady to catch a mouse
N ever too furry
E veryone just loves him
Y es, I love him too.

Dominic Mercer (12)
St Luke's High School, Barrhead

Terminology

I don't know much about English,
I think it sounds like jargon.

It must just be ironic,
Because I actually enjoy it.

I find it hard to spell the words,
I thought simile was a facial expression.

A statement is to say something,
To say something intelligent and clever.

Metaphor is spelt all wrong,
It should be 'f' and not 'ph'.

But most of all,
I cannot spell -

Onomatopoeia!

Lauren Heaney (12)
St Luke's High School, Barrhead

Fate

Upon the tall hill of Bahon village stand red roses,
These roses stand tall and do not fall,
Until dripping in blood.
A man is stood there right now,
Ready to scare, I wonder how?
Roses are a sign of death,
But how could someone lose their breath?
The man has written in the book of fate,
That 3 girls will be the ones he picks to hate.
But could these delicate roses drip with blood?
If so everyone will wonder how he could,
Hurt Katie Earl, Ellie Able and Sarah Tate,
Yet no one can change the book of fate.

Helen O'Brien (13)
St Nicholas Catholic High School, Northwich

You!

You
Your head is like a hollow drum
You
Your eyes are like spinning tops
You
Your nostrils are like onions
You
Your mouth is like flubber
You
Your hands are like chicken dippers
You
Your belly is like an 8-storey car park
You
Your legs are like ships' funnels
You
Your backside is like the Titanic.

Scott Prince (11)
St Nicholas Catholic High School, Northwich

What Can You Do With An Umbrella?

If you want to be a hockey star
But you don't have a stick wherever you are
Just look around for an umbrella
It doesn't matter lass or fella
If the game was a fight
You decide to camp overnight
To do all these things
Just remember to bring
Your *magical, mystical umbrella!*

Emily-May Walker (11)
St Nicholas Catholic High School, Northwich

Young Writers - Great Minds From Near And Far

My Dad . . .

My dad is round and chubby,
But his feet are rather grubby.
My dad's feet are very smelly,
Especially when they have been in his welly.
My dad's eyes are nice and brown,
And his nose is red like a clown.
My dad has a very large belly,
It wobbles when he laughs whilst watching telly.
My dad likes eating Indian food,
Especially when he's in the mood.
Unfortunately this has repercussions
And we all have to hide under the cushions.
My dad used to have a four-wheel drive,
That he used to drive like a maniac.
Then one day the wheel fell off
And we all had a panic attack.
My dad is an excellent cook,
He makes fantastic chips,
They're as huge as battleships.
My dad used to make a wicked spag bog,
But one day he dropped it and gave it to the dog.
And then the next morning the dog had the trots,
And then the dog had to go behind a log.
My dad is no fun at all,
In fact we thought he was rather boring.
When we went up to see him in his chair,
We found him snoring.
My dad has many faults,
And he seems to moan at me.
He is the greatest dad of all.
I love him.

Emma Phillips (11)
St Nicholas Catholic High School, Northwich

Houston, We Have A Problem

'Houston, we have a problem,'
I said in my cardboard spaceship,
Or instead of a spaceship
I could have a hat that's totally hip.

I could watch TV all day and night
Watching cardboard box TV
I could get a seat if I fight
In my cardboard house.

I could be a knight in brown armour
And save poor damsels in distress,
I could ride to sea on my boat
It truly would be a mess.

My brother says it's just a cardboard box,
But I know what it really is,
A time machine that can fly through time
But really it's his.

Grace Wells (11)
St Nicholas Catholic High School, Northwich

Football

There are different shapes and sizes,
People win them as prizes,
They get kicked, hit and thrown,
Dogs like them more than a bone.

Some are oval - some are round,
The crowds shout and make loud sounds,
Used for goals, penalties and aims,
All sorts of sports and different games.

Some are black and some are white,
Some are heavy, some are light,
Used by players large and small,
Girls and boys use them all.

Grace Ashcroft (11)
St Nicholas Catholic High School, Northwich

What If

(Based on 'What If' by Shel Silverstein)

'Last night, while I lay thinking here,
Some Whatifs crawled inside my ear
And pranced and partied all night long
And sang their same old Whatif song:'

Whatif Justin Timberlake swept me off my feet?
Whatif I turn into meat?
Whatif I trip and die?
Whatif I turn into an apple pie?
Whatif I can't stop sucking my thumb?
Whatif I don't like apple-flavoured buns?
Whatif I don't grow into a woman?
Whatif if start doing all the shouldn'ts?
Whatif I break my head?
Whatif I can't go to bed?
Whatif I visit Planet Zog?
Whatif I walk into a log?
'Everything seems swell, and then
The night-time Whatifs strike again!'

Lauren Stanton (11)
St Nicholas Catholic High School, Northwich

Poem

It shreds and cuts, it makes the grasshoppers hop.
It sounds like a motorbike.
Its blades are as sharp as scissors.
It may shred the flowers.
It may cut the sky.
It could cut your tie.
It could even cut your hair.
It drives around all day.
It cuts and shreds every insect.
Its teeth eat anything in sight.
It eats lots of grass and it likes to chomp on pests.

Annabelle Keaveny (11)
St Nicholas Catholic High School, Northwich

Dance Of Broken Misery

Corruption of a broken heart,
Stand and watch as the sky falls apart,
Bleeding down on the heads of the martyrs,
Locked away in a dance so farther down.

Staring at the ceiling as you walked into the black oblivion,
As the cracks in the sky fall into the face of decay.
And the sun sleeps, turning you into just a memory,
The memory of our dance of misery.

Trying to stitch a broken paper heart,
A disgrace of a world to fall apart.
Bleeding down on the barrel of a gun,
And locked away in a dance so farther down.

Pull the flawed sublime to the hands of time,
And those make-believe wings pulling you with the strings,
Of a day of suicide in that deep, black heart of mine.
Escape from the clutch of the Devil's claw.

Staring at the ceiling as you fade away into oblivion,
The cracks in the sky falling, turning into a face of decay.
While the sun still sleeps, turning you into just another memory,
A memory of our dance of broken misery.

Rachael Williams (11)
St Nicholas Catholic High School, Northwich

Death's Door

I am weak and old,
Please spare a penny for the poor,
The days are hot but the nights are cold,
I can't get on with my life anymore.
I am hungry and weak,
A penny or two could help me through,
For food is all I seek,
A penny . . . so much to me, so little to you.
I am weak and old,
Please spare a penny for the poor,
The days are hot but the nights are cold,
I am inches away from death's door!

I am weak and old,
Please give me a second thought,
You look at me and it's me you scold,
I wear no more than a vest and short,
Because I live on the street.
Please, a penny to you is not much at all,
I know I'm not elegant like the other people that you meet,
I beg you, I ask you, it's you that I call.
I am weak and old,
Please spare a penny for the poor,
The days are hot but the nights are cold,
I am only a knock away from death's door!

Samantha Roe (13)
St Nicholas Catholic High School, Northwich

I Am?

I am the floorboards you walk on
I am the magazine you read
I am the shed you go to
I am the bed that you need.

I am the door that you open
I am the chair on which you sit
I am the poster you gaze at
I am the bonfire which is lit.

I am the fence in the garden
I am also the gate
I am the trees in the woodland
I am also ornate.

I am sometimes soft
I am sometimes hard
I am many different shades
I am also card.

I am paper in a book
I am a boat on the sea
I am in everyone's life
But what might I be?

Alex Willemsen (11)
St Nicholas Catholic High School, Northwich

Guess Who?

It can cut the grass,
Or cut the sky,
It might even fly.
It can cut the carpet,
Or cut your hair,
Cut, shred and tear.

It's like a goat,
Loud, fat and has big teeth.
It can murder someone,
Splash, bang, splat!

It's like a train,
Such a big pain.
It can cut wood,
But not in mud.

It can chuck,
The whole world shook.
And it can vibrate,
Such a headache!

What is it?

Gabriella Gough (11)
St Nicholas Catholic High School, Northwich

Ice!

It is
Deep and white and yellow,
With little streams of sunlight
Within its bed.
Its frozen fingers touch the
Skin, freezing ice.
The stare of it is deadly.
The heat stops the
Frozen touch.
It's
Ice!

Andrew Jones (11)
St Nicholas Catholic High School, Northwich

My Life With Paper

I made a paper aeroplane with it before my teacher came into class,
I made a little ball with it, I made a great big pass,
I took it to my bedroom, I turned on my light,
I cut it up in different places, I customised a kite.

I woke up the next morning, no school today,
I sang, *'Hooray, hooray, no school today.'*
I rang up my mate, he said he would play out,
I picked up my paper and left without a doubt.
We had a great time sitting by the river,
At least today it didn't make me shiver.
We made a couple of paper boats, we had a little race,
Our boats floated down the river with a steady pace.

Matthew Whittaker (11)
St Nicholas Catholic High School, Northwich

In Search Of Freedom

(In memory of Anne Frank)

An eye that peers,
A heart that fears.

A knock on the door,
We just can't ignore.

A piercing scream,
Sounds in the dim.

And in the night,
They come to fight.

Hope flies away,
To the ocean's bay.

Nothing's left,
It looks like a theft.

Taken away,
Life ended today.

Aarti Daryanani (13)
San Silvestre School, Peru

In My Mind

I lift my gaze at the sound of feet
Reality patent in every heartbeat
My hidden shelter
My unveiled core
But nothing's real anymore

In my mind . . .
Thread by thread the web of emotion
Eternity and fantasy entwined
Step by step the path of elation
Until I stand in the borderline

In my mind . . .
Nothing's real
Nothing's wrong
This is why
I've been hiding here all along

And as I wander aimlessly
Through this maze, my mind's eye
I marvel at the only thing
That is only mine

Who am I?

Just a shadow, the truth of a lie . . .

Where am I?

In the deepest depths of my mind . . .

Angie Hanawa (12)
San Silvestre School, Peru

The Scent Of Past

She closed her eyes, and felt the scent,
Regardless of reality, to the past she went.
Unstoppable fingers caressed her hair,
As the warm, blue sheets embraced her chest.
Her warm, sad heart to her mind then said:
'Please guide me, teach me, to stay here again.'

He fought with swords and daggers and mud,
And never stopped feeding his sadness with blood.
His wounds were healed by her soft, dead hands,
The same that asked his death for a dance.
His desiring heart to his fists then said:
'I want her, I need her, to feel only my scent.'

She heard his stare, calling her from the night,
He was crying, dying, way too tired of the fight.
Her heart stopped beating, she lost all sight,
But his blood and his pain turned into her light.
Her calm, red lips to her eyes then said:
'He is my own sight now, I am his own stare.'

He held her tightly, and kissed her in his mind,
Laying on the ground, with the lonely moon he cried.
He had been her whole life, he was too her end,
Never in the present, always when he slept.
His soft, cruel sighs to her eyes then said:
'You belong to me now, in your life and death.'

Maria Laura Lizarzaburu (16)
San Silvestre School, Peru

Majorca

As I walk down the street
A jasmine yellow duck jumps out,
That day at the light blue pool
The clean smell of the chlorine made me want to dive in,
That night when we went out to party I was all dressed up.
As I ate my big brown steak that night,
My mum and dad were very happy,
As I wore my emerald top.
The disco beams glittered and rocked,
The lovely colours red, purple, yellow and lime made our faces glow.

Johnathan Walker
Stewarton Academy, Stewarton

Bonfire

The crackling of the bonfire,
The yellow glowing fire,
The glowing orange flames,
The black smoke floating in the air,
The fireworks fly around
The bang of the fireworks,
The gleam when the smoke clears.

Joe Stubbs (12)
Stewarton Academy, Stewarton

The Beach

The turquoise sea moves calmly up the beach,
The fine golden sand burnt my feet,
Tanned bodies jumping up and hitting the ball over the net,
The clear jellyfish lying on the hot, smooth sand ready to sting.
People lying on their sunbeds looking at the sun
                        through designer sunglasses.

Stephen Shaw (12)
Stewarton Academy, Stewarton

A Long Journey

The horse is galloping steady but fast
Over high walls and through the cloud's mast
He kicks his chestnut legs into the sky
Hearing his squeal to the birds that fly
Smelling his sweat that comes off in waves
His golden mane flowing in the wind
His hooves clattering like silver tins
He stands proud on jagged rocks
His tail swirling in golden locks.

He canters through a forest so dark
Something spooks him, he's off like a spark
Then he spots a waterfall
The water glittering like a diamond ball
He plunges into the aqua pool
Tasting the water sweet and cool
He starts at a walk and then a trot
The sun's bright rays making him feel hot
He starts to gallop along a sandy beach
Trying to get where he still can't reach
But at last he reaches his destiny
A giant herd grazing under a tree.

Emma Milligan (13)
Stewarton Academy, Stewarton

Christmas Tree

The tree is emerald green
The golden star shining bright
Scarlet tinsel, sapphire blue,
Ruby, violet lights that shine,
Indigo and silver wrapping paper
Snow-white fairy lights.
The sugar from the candy sticks,
The sound of Santa, ho! ho! ho!
The smell of red wine
The taste of milk and cookies.

Christopher Dinning (12)
Stewarton Academy, Stewarton

The Fairground

A luminous, blue roller coaster flies on the rails,
A carousel whizzes with blurred scarlet trails,
An ear-piercing scream comes from the ghost train,
Multicoloured fireworks burst like rain,
While the motorised goalie catches footballs,
Ruby-red lights flash round the food stalls,
The smell of hot dogs and burgers hangs around,
While an electric blue drop ride *slams* to the ground,
The sounds of the dark theme park fade from the dream
As the luminous, blue roller coaster fades from the scene.

Matthew Allison (12)
Stewarton Academy, Stewarton

Christmas Day

The red and gold glow of the gift tag stuck on the presents.
The face of the little kids as they see their gifts
The thought of what might be in them
The careful steps trying not to stand on them
What could be the most joyful Christmas ever
The taste of the sweets, the last chocolate from the Advent calendar
The smell of the new flowers for your mum
The pretend look from your dad acting like he likes his slippers.

Alistair Green (12)
Stewarton Academy, Stewarton

Las Vegas

The Las Vegas strip is flashing its colours
Diamond-white, golden-yellow and scarlet-red,
Glow through the strip like a raging fire,
The casinos *brrrring!* and *flash* when they win,
The people sing because they have won,
The glow in their eye says that they have won a million.

Colin Stapely (13)
Stewarton Academy, Stewarton

What Colour Is It?

It is like a bruise on my leg,
When I'm angry, it's the colour of my face,
My favourite fruit, a juicy grape,
My face when I've just run and I'm exhausted,
It's my favourite sweet Palma Violets,
Like a bunch of violets sitting in a field,
What colour is it?

Emily Poggi
Stewarton Academy, Stewarton

Firework Display

Bright! Bright! Bright! High in the sky.
Every colour you could imagine in different shapes and sizes,
And the feel of the wind hitting your face.
Suddenly, the fastest, most colourful sparkler shoots up,
And when it falls, the smell of the grey fumes coming off it.

Paul Stephen (12)
Stewarton Academy, Stewarton

Red Poem

The teacher raging in the class,
The blood dripping from the burst wound,
The cars stopping when they see the sign,
The blush on the girl's face,
The happiness of the champions,
The love between girls and boys.

Robbie McCreadie (12)
Stewarton Academy, Stewarton

Chinese New Year

Ruby, sapphire and golden lanterns
Are all over the place
Lemon-yellow, emerald-green and sea-blue dragons
Are prancing everywhere.

I can smell Chinese food,
It smells really wonderful,
A mixture of meats and vegetables
And very hot spices.

I can hear Chinese voices
Coming from the streets,
All the rabble and babble
Is very loud indeed.

All the wonderful colours,
So bright and amazing,
This is my description
Of Chinese New Year.

Gordon Burnett (13)
Stewarton Academy, Stewarton

The Football Game

The football game goes on and on,
I didn't think it would go for this long.
The referee's whistle kept going for ages,
All of the players playing their hardest.
The colour of the shining green pitch,
The sound of the roaring fans,
Waiting for their team to score again.
The golden sun beats down in the brightly lit up stand.
The sparkling pale blue strips against the devil-red ones.
The fans cheering on their heroes,
Excited in case their team puts one in the back
                              of the glittering white net.

Blair Smith (12)
Stewarton Academy, Stewarton

Circus

Acrobats swinging, high in the sky.
Brave fire-eaters light up the tent.
Strong men in tight, saffron lion skins,
The crowd cheers.
The clowns appear, crazily dressed
In scarlet red checks and azure stripes.
Magicians act formally and disappear in indigo smoke,
Stone grey elephants balance carefully on one leg.
Bright tigers patrol and dangerous lions
Are controlled by a tamer cracking his tough whip.
The children watch with their pink fluffy candyfloss
And multicoloured sweets.
The band finishes.
The show is over.
The acts march off in a sea of colour.

Ewan Baillie (12)
Stewarton Academy, Stewarton

Before The Match

Cheerful, confident, loyal fans,
Shouting and singing.
Red faces everywhere, to match their scarlet tops,
The golden sun beating down on the lush emerald pitch.
The cold wind slapping everyone in the face.
The fiery colours of yellow and red from the away support
The stomach-churning stench of golden, greasy pies and stale crisps.
Everyone intending to win.
The intense pressure from the opposition.
The killing anxiety and anticipation amongst the fans.
The last burst of chanting,
Then silence,
As the shiny, silver whistle is raised to the referee's mouth.

Kirsty McWilliam (12)
Stewarton Academy, Stewarton

Colours Of The Fairground

All the colours around the fair
Entertainers with bright, aqua hair
Haunted houses all grey and black
Children winning brown teddies at the coconut shack

Baby-pink candyfloss all fluffy and light
People walking around with colourful kites
The smell of burnt, black hot dogs on the grill
Foaming, pink ice cream giving you a chill

Lots of stalls selling many things
Necklaces of silver and golden rings
The leaf-green pitch of Beat the Goalie
Hook a prize and win a new dolly

Fluorescent roller coasters about fifty feet tall
Bric-a-brac for sale at the car boot stall
Scarlet dodgems zooming around
So many colours at the fairground!

Conor Nisbet (12)
Stewarton Academy, Stewarton

Christmas

The green, jaggy tree twinkles with golden tinsel.
Scarlet-red baubles glisten in the white lights.
We sit and listen to Christmas music.
During the frosted night, a red figure flies over the roof
And out of sight.
The oranges, reds and yellows of the burning fire
Glowing in the warm room reflect in the frosty window.
The golden turkey sizzles in the oven
Starting to form a crispy coating.
The white, frosty footprints melt away in the hall,
With the multicoloured paper lying on the floor.

Rachel Bow (12)
Stewarton Academy, Stewarton

At The Shows

Bright lights glow like crystals
In the cool, night sky
Money jingling in the pockets
Of the kids that run straight by
Ruby-red and golden-yellow rides
Spin and twirl around
Music blasting from every corner
Such a noisy sound
Children shouting and screaming
Running for every ride
As the sky gets darker
The sun begins to hide.

Rachael Sheach (12)
Stewarton Academy, Stewarton

Christmas Day

The wrapping paper being thrown around all red and gold.
Children jumping around with excitement in their PJs
Mum and Dad opening their presents slowly.
Brothers and sisters fighting over whose presents are best,
The smell of new presents around the house,
Also the smell of Xmas dinner being prepared.
The turkey coming out of the oven,
The rumbling of empty tummies waiting.
The clatter of pans,
Smelly neaps and tatties, that you always get.
But I just eat my turkey, that's the best!

Lindsay Richmond (12)
Stewarton Academy, Stewarton

Fairground

The funny clowns with aqua hair
The children running everywhere
The disco lights, golden and green
The magician disappearing or so it would seem

The haunted house with blood all over
The frosty ice cream like the White Cliffs of Dover
The sugar-pink candyfloss from the fair
Sticking to children with long hair

Childish screams from the red roller coasters
Lots of stalls with colourful posters
Stripy dodgems bashing into things
Stalls selling pretend diamond rings
Flashing lights on the merry-go-round
These are the joys of a busy fairground!

Greg Leyden (12)
Stewarton Academy, Stewarton

Hallowe'en

Ruby red devil costumes, wigs, hats and shoes.
Emerald-green face paints on kids.
Dressed as goblins, snakes and witches.
Pure white sheets over little boys and girls.
Amber shaded pumpkins sitting on the doorsteps.
People of all ages young and old
Carrying candy bags bursting with candy.
Black cats, plastic bats and lime green lamps
In the hands of angelic fairies.
This is Hallowe'en.

Briony Mitchell (12)
Stewarton Academy, Stewarton

Christmas Tree

The glowing of the Christmas tree
Presents Santa brings for you and me
The decorative lights around the street
Merry Christmas to the people you meet.

Sitting round the table ready to eat
When your mum brings through the golden meat
Unwrapping the presents to see what you've got
Things that your mum and dad have bought.

Out parting until late at night
The lights were still on so it was bright
Going to bed to wait till next day
Which would be the 26th, my birthday.

Darren Ronaldson (12)
Stewarton Academy, Stewarton

Chinese New Year

Extravagant dancing down the street
Traditional food, the aroma so sweet
Ruby, lime, sapphire, colours so mellow
Scarlet, avocado, orange and yellow

Music and babble fills the air
Not a space in the crowd left spare
Colourful decorations hang so high
Multicoloured dragons swish and sway by

Chinese New Year, what a sight!
Some of the dragons will give you a fright
When performers arrive the crowd go mad
No one could possibly be sad.

Ruairidh McMillan (12)
Stewarton Academy, Stewarton

The Stables

The cars parked along the terracotta stones
In all different shades of the rainbow
The rusty, iron gate tightly closed
And behind it, the world I loved most, the stables.

The horses all lined up in rows
Ready to be brushed and cleaned
The coloured cobs, duns, bays and greys
Stood tall in the sun and gleamed.

The smell of shampoo, hoof oil and sprays
As well as hayledge and straw
Sawdust, treats, apples and cabbage
And fiery carrots, crispy and raw.

The sound of hooves in all kinds of rhythms
Canter, trot and walk
The horses whinnying contentedly
Listening to their riders laugh and talk.

Their golden, black and coloured manes
Soft and sleek like silk
The golden hay, crispy and tough
The powdery sawdust pouring like milk.

The colourful lead ropes, rugs and numnahs
In sunshine yellow, lavender and aqua-blue
Such a bright wave of colours up at the stables
I can't wait to get back there, can you?

Caitlin Burns (12)
Stewarton Academy, Stewarton

The Death Of Love

Why are they fighting?
Why won't they stop?
Please just stop it,
Stop, I said, stop!

Screaming and shouting
Pushing and shoving,
Leave each other alone,
Please don't stop loving.

What are you doing?
Take your hands off her,
Let go, let go,
Take your hands off her.

Why did you hit her?
What has she done?
She's crying out for you,
Don't go . . . he's gone.

Why doesn't he care?
Your bruised, frail body,
Shaking and quivering
You are alone, there's nobody.

Weaker and weaker,
You begin to fade,
Fighting for your life,
Where is the love you gave?

What can I do?
Nothing but watch
'Help me,' you cry,
I can do nothing but watch.

What did you do?
You did nothing but love.

Laura Marszalek (12)
Stratford-upon-Avon High School, Stratford-upon-Avon

On A Summer's Day

The sun is high
And the breeze still blows
Through the flowers
Rows on rows
By your grave on a summer's day

The harsh light shines
Off marble stone
Besides the birds
I sit alone
By your grave on a summer's day

I thought I saw you
One dismal day
But you were gone
When I looked away
By your grave on a summer's day

Every day I've come
And continue I will
To visit this place
So calm and still
By your grave on a summer's day

The tears I cry
Land like pearls
Ever since you
Left this world
By your grave on a summer's day

I've come again
You lie there
Deep in the earth
I stand and stare
At your grave on a summer's day.

Louie Kenyon-Crockett (13)
Stratford-upon-Avon High School, Stratford-upon-Avon

Clouded Minds

Her footsteps fill the empty lane,
She is off to end her terrible pain,
This world can be so cruel sometimes,
So much murder, hate and crimes.

A sharp blade she draws,
To the ground she falls,
Blood spills from her throat,
Onto her suicide note.

Depression and pain,
Never again,
Her soul;
So cold.

This is all she wanted,
To be free . . .

Bethan Jones (13)
Stratford-upon-Avon High School, Stratford-upon-Avon

What If That Was Me?

Walking the dark and desolate streets,
I saw a man in tattered, shabby rags,
He looked starving, with hollow eyes,
I just walked on by,
But then I thought, *how did he get here,*
Far from his home?
What would I do if that was me?

Trying to see myself through his eyes,
It's working, I see, hear, touch and taste it,
I sit here in inexplicable sadness,
I see myself walk by.

Alice Kinoulty (12)
Stratford-upon-Avon High School, Stratford-upon-Avon

Paradise

There is a gorgeous place,
That shines among the stars,
That beholds every sound on Earth,
All the way to Mars.

The water there is warm,
And pleasant to touch with hands,
The waves are lapping in the sand,
And making little dams.

The mountains in the sky,
Have waterfalls glowing,
Pouring into glittery seas,
That ripples when it's snowing.

The trees are young and slender,
With bark as tough as steel,
And buds that bloom everywhere,
Blossom to appeal.

The bushes are crisp and green,
That wrinkle if you stare,
The vines pushing towards the sun,
Make the island floor bare.

I've told you everything to know,
About this lovely place,
Clear waters and blue skies,
That smiles upon your face!

Christina Mann (13)
Stratford-upon-Avon High School, Stratford-upon-Avon

Pandora's Box

There once was a girl called Pandora
And everyone chose to ignore her
So she opened her box
Undid all the locks
And now the world is much poorer.

Stuart Macaulay (13)
Stratford-upon-Avon High School, Stratford-upon-Avon

The Morning Of Summer

In the early morning hours
Of this soon to be
Hot summer's day
A bird awakes
To the sun's beautiful rays.

The dewdrops on the leaves
Begin to disappear
Ready for the day to begin
To listen to the children cheer.

Inside the house
Tiny footsteps patter through
As the sound of the alarm rings
People awake to start the day new.

The boiling of the kettle
The popping of the toaster
Children running everywhere
As school gets closer.

In the early morning hours
Of this soon to be
Hot summer's day
Such a rush to get prepared
For the rest of the day.

Chloe Guy (13)
Stratford-upon-Avon High School, Stratford-upon-Avon

Footstep In The Wind

Where once the sunlight beamed
The paw of darkness holds
Through an eternal pitch-black dream
The secret of a child will never be sold.

The footstep of a man
Left in the wind
Printed to a harsh, cold night
Where the Devil once sinned.

Let yourself fly
Through the ever-changing cry
Explore the dreams you never had
Such things couldn't make you sad.

The call of a jackal
The blunt, sweet air
However can this darkness comfort you
When all they say is share?

The footstep gets further
Sand blows the pain away
Now the sea shall fall
While the coral will sway.

As the dawn of day comes
The footstep disappears
Wind takes the man away
The moon in the sky, no longer here.

Ben Parry (13)
Stratford-upon-Avon High School, Stratford-upon-Avon

VE Day

Fighting has come to an end,
Families and friends are reunited,
Fun and laughter fill the streets again,
As parties are held throughout the land.

Memories of comrades we will never see again,
Are still there in our minds,
As evacuees return home,
To see buildings demolished into rubble.

Homes return to normal;
Blackout curtains gone,
And air raid sirens ceased,
Flags fill the streets.

Peace at last,
6 years have finally paid off,
Flags are raised to celebrate;
    'Our victory!'

Charlotte Howdle (13)
Stratford-upon-Avon High School, Stratford-upon-Avon

Bannoffee Pie

Sweet sensation
Naughty treat
Sticky surprise
Mouth-watering moment
Crumbly morsel
Mini memento
Caramel temptation.

Louisa Heyworth (13)
Stratford-upon-Avon High School, Stratford-upon-Avon

Think

I'm all alone now,
They've all gone,
I'm battered and bruised
But my general says, 'We've won.'

I sit alone in my trench
And stare up at the sky;
The tranquil, blue mist
And I ask myself, *why?*

I've lost my friends,
I've lost my family too
Because of a stupid mistake,
Who is to blame? Could it be you?

I hear a distant scream,
A small tear creeps down my cheek,
I feel so alone,
I feel so weak.

I've lost my mum, my dad too,
I sit alone, feeling the pain.
I just don't understand,
Has anyone made any gain?

It will haunt me all my life,
Every night I wake to the screams.
All the people I have killed
Float peacefully in my dreams.

But what was it for?
Thousands killed in one blink.
Please take one second for them
And just *think . . .*

Emma Stubbs (12)
Stratford-upon-Avon High School, Stratford-upon-Avon

Guilt

What is this feeling?
My stomach aches inside
I'm trembling
But I know I can't hide.

This anxiety
Pouring into the pits of my body
From head to toe
I have to tell.

I know I shouldn't
I don't know why
Resist but I couldn't
I had to lie.

My palms are sweating
My breathing is deep
It's so hard forgetting
What I did last week.

Zoe Lucock (12)
Stratford-upon-Avon High School, Stratford-upon-Avon

Little Bean

(Based on the book 'Blue Moon' by Julia Green)

A small, worthless blob,
Some feelingless cells,
Becoming something more,
The end? No one can tell.

It's out of the question,
She's only fifteen!
Yet nothing can stop her,
It's her little bean.

Bar the baby inside her,
She's all alone.
No one understands her,
Should she keep it for her own?

She can't have an abortion,
They can't force her to.
It's her little bean,
What would you do?

Victoria Lyon (13)
Stratford-upon-Avon High School, Stratford-upon-Avon

It's Coming

It's coming,
The time for him to go,
He steps up on the platform,
This is the end as he knows.

The waves crash below him,
Like a violent shark attack,
He pulls himself over the bar,
The wind blows on his back.

He looks over the cliff,
Tears trickle down his cheek,
His life is now pointless,
It's all so very bleak.

He looks at the scars on his wrist,
And cries a little more,
And gets ready to aim for the water,
And get washed up on the shore.

Although he was about to jump,
He took the time to sit,
And think a bit about this,
He could not do it.

He turns around about to get down,
But the light is so dim,
He slips off the bar,
This fatal night kills him.

Gabby May (12)
Stratford-upon-Avon High School, Stratford-upon-Avon

The Thundercloud

I was angry with my wife
Like a witch, she ruined my life
I was angry with my friend
My hate, it did not end

And I heated it with the boom of my voice
Noon and night it brewed and brewed
And I cooled it with the black of their hearts
Noon and night it brewed and brewed

It grew evermore powerful day by day
Till it bore a cloud so ferocious and grey
And my enemies were not aware
Of what anger, it was sure to scare

And out came the cloud of smoke
Strike 1 to the heart of hers, now broke
Strike 2 to the head of his, now smashed
Their relationship, like mine, now crashed.

Pete Hurst (13)
Stratford-upon-Avon High School, Stratford-upon-Avon

Loneliness

Loneliness is like no one cares;
Loneliness is an unwanted feeling,
Everything is really bad.
Loneliness is like you want revenge;
Loneliness is like everyone's gone.
Loneliness is being friendless -
All your family have gone.
No one here . . . no one.

Thomas Barron (12)
The King's Academy, Middlesbrough

The Bird!

I saw a bird in the sky
It was very, very high
I stopped and stared for just a while
And then popped out a little smile
The bird was big and long and loud
I looked and looked and looked around
I didn't know where the noise was coming from
So I just stood and wondered.

I thought this bird was so amazing
I just stood there gazing
I was so amazed
To see a bird like this
This bird was big and long and loud
I even went home thinking of the sound
All that night it was in my head
Even when I went to bed!

Laura Noble (12)
The King's Academy, Middlesbrough

Myrtle

(In memory of my late dog Myrtle)

A dog is for life, or so we are told,
I know it is true, for my dog is cold

She had a good life, was my friend and my mate,
She grew up with me. Our life was great.

Chocolate bar . . . that was her shade,
With big, brown eyes. With me she played.

We were a good pair as we added on years,
But her passing on made me cry tears upon tears.

Maybe you think that now I am sad,
But for her fun life I really am glad!

Alyssa Bodycombe (13)
The King's Academy, Middlesbrough

Las Vegas

In Las Vegas,
The buildings are high,
If you don't win,
You're sure to sigh.

In Las Vegas,
There is a lot to win,
If you win lots,
Your old house will be in the bin.

All hotels are different,
There is a lot to see,
There are lots of people,
It's a good place to be.

With dolphins and tigers,
And really scary rides,
It is so amazing,
You'll escape from your insides.

The Stratosphere Tower,
Is the tallest thing in the city,
You see all the lights from the top,
Using all the electricity.

Matthew Kirby (13)
The King's Academy, Middlesbrough

Love

Love can be bold
Love can be strong
Love can also be wrong
Yes I love you
But you don't love me
My heart's broken for eternity
I had this girl, this girl had me
We were made for each other
It was our *destiny*.

Ben Nixon (12)
The King's Academy, Middlesbrough

Into The Light

I'm a dead body,
Deep underground,
Down where I am,
There is no sound.

I lie down here,
Day after day,
My life is over,
The price I must pay.

It's now I wonder,
Was I so bad?
Cos where I am now,
It's just so sad.

I miss my family,
I miss my best friend,
And now I realise,
My life must end.

I see the golden stairs,
I see the bright, white light,
And what I see now is,
The most beautiful sight.

Alexandra Miller (12)
The King's Academy, Middlesbrough

Alone!

Pretty, soft dog, sitting and hurt,
Alone, no home, no food, only sleep.
Alone without family,
Pretty scared,
Fur as cold as snow,
Pushing through bars trying to find home,
Painful and crinkly eyes, sad.

Waiting for a person to pick me up,
Softly I cry making noises as sweet as a song.

Amy B Bell (12)
The King's Academy, Middlesbrough

Electric Storm

The sky is black as ebony
The air so heavy and dull
A sudden flash, a sudden bang
With volts the atmosphere's full

Crashing to the ground
Soaring through the sky
A sudden flash, a sudden bang
What a feast for our eyes

Flashes, bangs and crashes
Fire in the sky
A sudden flash, a sudden bang
Thunderbolts way up high

A chink of light shines through the clouds
As the birds start to fly
A lull of peace and quiet
A prism in the sky.

Sarah Pinkney (12)
The King's Academy, Middlesbrough

The Night-Time Walk

Brown and blonde dogs
Rooting through the snow
Want to play
Have some fun

Trees move gently
The breeze blowing slowly
Through the branches
Bare twigs covered in snow

The night is bright
Before the darkness comes
Home fires burn
Home safe and warm.

Eleanor Trueman (12)
The King's Academy, Middlesbrough

Alone

Lonely,
Abandoned,
Isolated is
What
Lonely
Feels like.
It is lonely. A
Starless night is
Loneliness. Loneliness
Is an empty room with
No escape.
Loneliness
Is a crowd
Of strangers.
Loneliness
Is neglected.
Loneliness
Is unaccompanied.
Loneliness is
Desolated. Loneliness
Is like being far away
Or distant from family
And friends. Loneliness is
Like being taken away from
People. Loneliness is like being trapped . . .

Louise McGill (12)
The King's Academy, Middlesbrough

Alone

I'm alone
But there's a
Big crowd, I don't
Know anyone, how
Can it be?
I feel so un-
Alive.
How can it
Be? It can be.
No one here loves

Me   I feel I like   a tiny
Un-   loved strain   of
Grass,   lost in the   breeze
Of the wind.   It's
Not   a nice feel-   ing
But   that's how I   feel
In   this big, mixed up   place.

I don't like it.
I want to go home, by the
Warm, soothing fire, but I
Can't, I can't give in, not now,
not after I've gone sooo far! Just standing
here. How
can it be?
It can be.
I am
Unknown.

Bethany Elenor (12)
The King's Academy, Middlesbrough

Riddle

You can put ink on him to keep records,
Or just to take a note,
He can come in different colours,
And can fit into your coat.

He is sometimes used for calendars,
But he's not as strong as the lord,
The lord is his older brother,
His name is cardboard.

You can turn him into an aeroplane,
Or into a boat,
It can be quite fun,
But you'll find that he can't float.

As you can see he's very useful,
I'll give you one more thing,
For these words that you are reading,
Are printed on him.

Katie Leggett (12)
The King's Academy, Middlesbrough

Alone

Loneliness is like an empty room,
It fills you up with evil and gloom.
It will fill you full of fear,
It will make you drop a tear.
Loneliness is like an empty bowl,
It drains the happiness from your soul.
Loneliness is the biggest fright,
Loneliness is a starless night.
By yourself with nothing to do,
You wish someone was with you.
It will make you want to cry,
It will make your heart go dry.
Away from someone you really know,
The loneliness does nothing but grow.

Perry Frost (12)
The King's Academy, Middlesbrough

Young Writers - Great Minds From Near And Far

The Mythology of Dragons

Dragons swoop,
Dragons glide,
Dragons don't feel,
They do not hide.

They have no fear,
They do not cry,
They have no sympathy
For neither you nor I.

Dragons won't listen,
Dragons don't speak,
They spurt out flames
Of tremendous heat.

Dragons are hollow,
They do not grin,
They break the rules,
They only sin.

Dragons don't sleep,
Dragons fly,
Dragons don't grieve,
They do not die.

Emma Cooksey-Artley (12)
The King's Academy, Middlesbrough

The River's Miseries

He gently trickles down the bank,
Over the bumpy surface,
Through the mysterious woods
Till he meets the Sleeping Willow,
She soothingly hums a sweet lullaby,
Yet he dances and prances on by,
At night you can hear his desperate cry,
For he can never stop to hear the end of his lullaby.

Cheryl Patterson (12)
The King's Academy, Middlesbrough

Other Than You

I'm feeling so fragile
My heart's torn in two
Why can't I love somebody
Other than you?

My problems would vanish
My heart would repair
And I would stop wishing
For you to be there

The tears on my pillow
Would cease to exist
And I'd stop dreaming
About those times when we kissed

I'd forget all those memories
And reasons I cried
Forget how you played me
Forget how you lied

But my heart is still broken
And you made it break
Shattered completely
More than I can take

I want to hate you
Make you suffer like me
But I love you too much
So I'm setting you free

Life would be easier
I'd make it through
If I loved somebody
Other than you!

Liam Bishop (13)
The King's Academy, Middlesbrough

Past It

I can't find my way home,
I'm just an old loner,
I'm supposedly one of a kind,
Stated by my owner.

I'm incapable of lifting my feet,
To make a few last strides,
But my legs are so clumsy they fail to shift,
I'm thinking my owner lied.

The end is coming soon,
But the remainder I intend to live,
With happy thoughts, you know the sort,
But trying to think with this old brain,
Is starting to bring me down.

My owner's really my child,
Just think that I'm past it,
But behind this frail and withered body,
I'm a young flower of intelligence and wit.

I may be a little slow,
But what's wrong with that?
The age bug catches everyone,
It's like being hit with a bat.

When you finally get hit,
It's not some gentle tap,
It's a great big whack,
That you can't turn back!
But I would if I could!

My body isn't up to scratch,
But my experience and wisdom,
No young one could match . . .

Lauren Kane (12)
The King's Academy, Middlesbrough

My Baby Brother

I remember the day when my mother,
Told me I was going to have a new baby brother,
My sister and I cried with delight,
Over his name we started to fight,
My mum's tummy was getting bigger and bigger . . .

I thought about my brother in my mum's tum,
We waited and waited for the big day to come,
At last came the day when my brother was born,
He had arrived!

I'll always remember the first time I saw him,
From that day on we always adore him,
At first all he did was eat and sleep,
And then later he started to creep,
He started to walk before he was one,
Then came his first birthday,
Where had that year gone?

Emily Morris (12)
The King's Academy, Middlesbrough

Poem On The Twin Towers

On Tuesday 11th September
Everyone can remember
What happened to the Twin Towers
That fell down in a few hours
Everyone was scared
And adults just cared
For young children who weren't theirs

So September 11th was the worst day
And all anyone can say
On Tuesday 11th September
We can all remember
What happened to the Twin Towers
That fell down in a few hours . . .

Ryan Foster
The King's Academy, Middlesbrough

My Little Friend

My tiny fur ball black and white,
Runs around late at night.

Eats her treats,
Her tiny sweets.

She'll run miles in her little wheel,
And moves quickly like a seal.

Her cage is her home,
It's shaped like a dome.

In the day she'll sleep,
With her bedding in a heap.

She's part of the family,
She squeaks at us happily.

She's my little hamster,
Nibbles!

Leanne Spence (13)
The King's Academy, Middlesbrough

Crazy Ocean

The sky is cerulean
As the sea twirls in turquoise
The power of the white waves swing
Ocean starts to curl around
The strength of the windy wave
The longer it travels the greater it gets
The sea grows angry
Feelings
Bottled up rage
Like a wild child.

As the sea lets out emotionally
And the ocean calms down, it goes bright blue.

Maryam Rasool (13)
The King's Academy, Middlesbrough

September 11th

Spending money
Having fun
Nobody knew
They'd have to run

Down came the towers
Darting like rain
Screams and shouts
Oh, the pain

Fire and flames
Letting out smoke
Children getting lost

Bits of plane
On the floor
We didn't get a chance
To get out the door

People were dying
More than tonnes
People were crying
To have lost their loved ones

This is what happened
In New York City
Oh it was
A tragic pity

Why did this happen?
What was their crime?
This is what happens
From time to time

Locked up in prison
Bin Laden and gang
All because of the
Explosive bang!

Ravinder Singh (13)
The King's Academy, Middlesbrough

The Story Of My Curse

This dreadful curse happened
That day in the shops would haunt me forever
That old lady as she beckoned

I warily went over, as she lifted her hooded cloak
She spoke to me in Greek
I had no idea what she meant

However, I was soon to find out . . .

When I looked into the mirror I could not cry
I could not scream
Help!

This carried on for years
On and on it went
This stupid, dreaded curse!

No more crying you will find
For now it's in the past
I'm now married with two children, and a husband who is kind

Let this be a lesson to you, don't go to awful strangers
For you may end up worse off than me
And end up never being happy

I'm glad that old hag hasn't ruined my life
She's helped me on my way
To living a carefree life.

The English translation from the Greek she spoke:
*From this day forward on the eighteenth of every other month you will go
as green as a turtle until you marry your one true love before your
twenty-fifth birthday. After that this curse will be lifted. However, if you
fail, it will be upon you forever and ever.*

Emma Brady (12)
The King's Academy, Middlesbrough

Teenagers

There was a group of 15-year-olds hanging around,
Violence and vandalism is what they were bound.

They went into a nearby shop and bought some eggs,
And that's when we saw we were about to be egged.

They threw an egg at every window that they saw,
Hard-boiled, poached eggs, others and raw.

All the neighbours started dialling nine-nine-nine,
Soon after the police were on the line.

But very daft people these teenagers were,
They saw a policewoman and ran up to her.

'Guilty! Guilty! Guilty!' they cried.
The policewoman put them in handcuffs and sighed.

'That's more teenagers rounded up,' she said.
She took them to a prison cell and put them in its bed.

'What a day! What a day! But it's over, hooray!
If children would behave as they did in my day.'

Daniel McCrae (12)
The King's Academy, Middlesbrough

Motorbikes

M otorbiking is the best motor sport in existence,
O r maybe it's not a sport, it's a passion,
T o be a motorcyclist is to be gifted,
O ften people fall off and lose their lives but yet,
R iders still carry on riding even though they know what
     could happen
B ecause there is nothing more fun,
I t's an incredible buzz to go fast on a motorcycle so
K awasakis, Ducatis and all other makes of bikes are still being
     sold by the million,
E very rider shares a passion and a friendship,
S o get out and ride.

Nathan Hutchinson (12)
The King's Academy, Middlesbrough

Bubbles

Bubbles flowing
Bouncing along
Getting smaller
And smaller
Going far away
Then reappearing again
Floating like see-through windows
Landing on the grass
Crisping through
The shiny flowers
The bubbles pop
Like a bomb
One by one
The bubbles won't be there
Forever
Blink your eyes
It's gone forever.

Sara Kendall (13)
The King's Academy, Middlesbrough

Lonely House

Blue house like the sea
Broken windows fresh to see
Scary birds rattle along
Knocking on the rooftop
Lonely house with spiders creeping along the floor
Spider spied on the door
Creeping dust, pictures peeling off the blinking wall
Old, peeling paint dropping off the wall
Fancy, old chimney crumbling, bit by bit.
Bright sky everywhere
Night sky, spooky air
Low, squeaking echo in the night gloom.

Sarah Janes (12)
The King's Academy, Middlesbrough

Best Buddies!

I have a best friend,
She's one of a kind,
Her name is Sammy,
It's like we can read each other's mind!

We're in all the same classes,
In the very same school,
She's the best friend ever,
She is *so* cool!

She's my best buddy; she's my best mate,
We hang out at break,
We have the greatest time,
And even have a secret handshake!

We'll get the same job,
We'll stick together,
We'll stay best buddies,
For ever and ever!

She's my best friend,
She's my best mate,
She's my best buddy,
Each other we'll never hate!

Rebecca Stewart (12)
The King's Academy, Middlesbrough

Angel Of The North

As it stands there,
All alone,
Watching the cars,
Go by,
Seeing people,
Everywhere.
Sometimes happy,
Sometimes sad,
Sometimes lonely,
Sometimes not.
It stands there,
Beautiful as can be.
It's not a bird,
It's not a tree.
It's an angel with wings,
A sweet melody it sings.
Every night, every day,
Nobody there to play.
Is this the end of the Angel of the North?
Will it be here in a few years' time?

Adam Robinson (12)
The King's Academy, Middlesbrough

My Love Story

He was my life,
The sun, moon and stars,
He kept me going,
But now he has gone,
Stay and listen to my sad tale.

It was like a magnificent dream,
He came on a summer's breeze,
And took me away,
Into a fantasy land.

He showed me the world,
From a different point of view,
I felt that nothing could pull me down,
Had I much more to learn?

He took me and sat me on a cloud,
And we looked through Heaven's gates,
He said, 'I love you,'
I was almost in tears.

Then the lightning came,
He tried to shelter me but was focusing on something else,
On the 'angel' higher above,
Then he was gone.

Suddenly I fell straight down to the ground,
I couldn't see anyone around me,
All I could see was him,
But he will never see me again.

Lana Walker (12)
The King's Academy, Middlesbrough

A Bad Decision

The night was still
And so were we,
Quietly whispering under the tree.

We rolled the tobacco,
Everything was ready,
In went the cigarette, all was steady.

And out of the dark
Came a striking sound,
An acrid smell was all around.

A cloud of smoke
Puffed into the air,
At that point in time no one did care.

We sat there for hours
Puffing away,
Till sickness came over us making us sway.

I started to walk
But my legs wouldn't let me,
How did that white stick make me feel so empty?

I realise now
My decision was wrong,
My mum and dad had been right all along.

If the police found out
That I'd been smoking Regal,
I'd be in big trouble for it is illegal.

Madeleine Brown (12)
The King's Academy, Middlesbrough

Snake

It slips and slides
Across the floor,
Looking like a stick,
It moves in
Such a special
Way,
You'd have
To be quick
For its trick.
Slowly but steadily
It moves along,
It sees its prey
And quickly it's
Gone. It's off again,
Moving along,
With its hunger satisfied,
It then reaches its large, own
Nest. Then it curls up
As it goes to bed.
It dreams
About what
It's going to do.
Slip, slide, eat,
Sleep is what
It's going to do.

James Craig (12)
The King's Academy, Middlesbrough

My Little Brother

My brother's a nuisance
He's a right pest
He annoys everyone
Mum says he's a test

No biscuits in the barrel
Finger marks on the door
There are crumbs on the sofa
Mud on the floor

We all hear a smash
Glass in the sink
Of course it was Harry
Puts mum on the brink

When he gets told off
He goes in a strop
Dad gets so angry
The vein's gonna pop

Of course he denies it
Says, 'It wasn't me.
Me? Break a glass?
That could never be.'

Despite that I love him
I have to in a sort of way
We get on alright
I suppose he is OK.

George Robinson (12)
The King's Academy, Middlesbrough

The Lion

He runs with a bounce
Along African plains
Over all the animals
The lion reigns

Strong and mighty
With teeth like spears
Ready to pounce
On anything it hears

He watches for animals
To tear apart
If they are aware
The animals will dart.

He watches his kingdom
Protecting his ground
When predators come near
He's always around

The lion watches
Happy with what he's done
He stands on his rock
And dares you to come.

Craig Runcieman (12)
The King's Academy, Middlesbrough

The Boil On My Nose

It's super-duper big,
It's red and yellow,
How do I cope?
Well, I try to be mellow!

Many people have boils,
But not like mine,
Mine's extraordinary,
I can see it all the time!

It's sprouted a hair,
This boil on my nose,
It's grown so long,
It tickles my toes!

I've tried to squeeze it,
It just won't pop,
It's really tempting,
I really can't stop!

This story's about,
The boil on my nose,
I just can't stand it,
I hope it soon goes!

Yuuuck!

Rachel Leatherland (12)
The King's Academy, Middlesbrough

Pretending To Be Me

I love to pretend to be myself
It's harder than I thought
I even stack things the same on my shelf
I buy things I've already bought

I say things that I always say
My friends think it's normal I suppose
I walked the same way home today
I even wear my own clothes

I put my own shoes on and brush my hair
The same way that I'd do
And they are very comfortable my underwear
And no one even knew.

I talk just the way I'd talk
And go where I would go
I'd talk to the people who talk to me
And say secrets only I would know

I do a good job sometimes
And everyone believes it's me
They don't know I'm not myself
But only pretending to be

So you'll never know next time
Who or what you see
I often pretend to be like myself
It's fun pretending to be me!

Jessica Duffy (12)
The King's Academy, Middlesbrough

A Little Hut

There is a little hut,
On a mud bank it sits.
Five people live there,
Their life is the pits.

They wake up every morning,
No light in their eye.
What a misery they think,
They wish they could die!

They go out to work,
In the harvest so gold.
Hacking the corn,
But they're getting too old.

But if this job will pay for us,
And all the rest of our family,
Then it must do, for all our life,
Is spent on the fields for you and me.

So help me, Lord,
Through this day.
I can't go on,
Yet for our family we must pay.

When we get home we will see,
A nice home with our family.
And well so far it'll do for us,
And we'll all sit down and have some tea.

Jessica Jones (12)
The King's Academy, Middlesbrough

The Swan

She glided softly like a gilded ghost,
Elegant and graceful, a ballet dancer of the ice,
Her perfect posture and swift, supple dance,
For anyone watching she could entice.

She seemed as if she was wearing an invisible crown,
Her gentle magnificence drifted through the air,
Her slender body shimmered as she crossed the lake,
Homeward bound towards her lair.

She appeared again from her home followed by her babies,
Approach this regal beauty now if you dare,
For she is a protective mother,
Touch her cygnets and beware.

The warm, summer evening gently draws to an end,
The sun is sleepily slipping away and evening beckons the moon,
The swan and her cygnets slowly head home,
Whilst the darkness murmurs a tune . . .

Megan Hudson (11)
The King's Academy, Middlesbrough

The Exam Hall

The exam hall, a silent, deathly area
Papers turning, pencils scratching
Teachers patrolling the rows upon rows
Laughing and chatting together
Pupils more tense than Michael Jackson in court
The tapping sound of your brain clicking
Your heartbeat bouncing like an insane bouncy ball
Your mind clock ticking, clicking away the seconds
Then you get to a question. What is the answer?
'Stop!' the teacher screams. The exam is finished
We leave the hall to find out another exam!
You just get the answer and your paper is snatched away.

Tony Robinson (14)
The King's Academy, Middlesbrough

9/11

American citizens,
At work, home or school,
Stopped for 2 minutes,
Because of the terrorist fools.

Viewers watched with horror,
Only one thing they knew,
With all the smoke, fire and ash,
That survivors will be few.

People ran away,
Being chased by debris and rubble,
Pieces of the planes came crashing down,
Fire-fighters on the double.

Thousands of casualties,
One candle for each,
Never even knew,
About the terrorist breach.

If only one crash can shake the world,
Then forever this story will be told,
And in that moment,
The world turned cold,
We knew a war was about to unfold.

Then people realised,
The radiant god of light,
Who killed the darkness and banished the night,
I have nothing but one thing to say,
God bless the USA.

Lewis de Andrade (13)
The King's Academy, Middlesbrough

The Unfairness Of An Unfair Life

When I was younger, my life was good,
With all my family, doing as I should.
In the right environment, my life began,
Then my dad, he went and ran.

Then I got pulled out, and dumped somewhere,
Nothing is right, *I'm pulling out my hair!*
The neighbours are noisy, I can't get rest,
And at school, I just can't do my best.

Everything is just so messed up, but I've learned to deal,
With the confusion, now I'm digging in my heel.
I *want* it better, I *want* out,
I *want* it back, I *want* to shout!

It's been four years, I've kept control,
But now I'm off, I'm on a roll!
I'll sort this out, it'll be so great,
Because this life I'm living, I simply hate!

I'll get us moved, we'll live in harmony,
We'll all be happy, just wait, you'll see.
But for now we'll wait, we can only hope,
Things will look up, we might just cope.

Samantha Wanless (12)
The King's Academy, Middlesbrough

Great Expectations - Miss Havisham

Miss Havisham's home,
Is old and dusty,
It's full of cobwebs and mice,
Don't ever go there because it's not pleasant or nice.

Its old bricks,
Filthy stairs,
Really ugly, wooden chairs,
Have all been there many years,
And she will not clean because she has no cares.

All her clocks have stopped at twenty to nine,
She says, 'Whose heart's broken? Mine, mine, mine.'
Miss Havisham is sad from being left at the altar,
You never know, her honeymoon might have been in Gibraltar.

The only person she has left in the world,
Is the stubborn young girl Estella.
Miss Havisham brought her up to hate all boys,
So now Estella treats all of them like toys.

Miss Havisham dies at the end of the story,
Just after Pip has left the room,
She sets on fire and screams and shouts,
Pip tries to save her but she doesn't survive.
So that was the end of Miss Havisham.

Emma Hill (13)
The King's Academy, Middlesbrough

9/11

9am Manhattan in rush hour,
They were about to be hit by a lot of power.
People set off on a normal plane.
They weren't to know that they wouldn't come back again.

9.30am the first plane struck
Down came showers of rubble and muck.
Then again another crash came,
At first they didn't know who to blame.

Screaming, terror, confusion all around,
Then the Twin Towers came crashing to the ground.
It was later revealed that it was the Al Qaeda group,
Osama bin Laden and his troops.

The search for bin Laden still goes on,
Where oh where has he gone?
On that day many people rose to Heaven,
On the day that was 9/11.

Matthew Nixon (12)
The King's Academy, Middlesbrough

Untitled

Look at that weirdo over there
Sitting in the corner without a care.
He's got strange glasses and ginger hair.
Who would really care if I hit him here or there?
I'll rob his new shoes, who cares if it's not fair?
I mean, look, he's a weirdo, who would care?
I'll rob your fags and all your money,
I'll laugh in your face, I think it's funny.
Look at you, you're a disgrace.
That boy's not a fighter, I'll go tax his lighter.
What if he bites me? Then he will have to fight me.
In my eyes he's just a little faggot,
An empty space.

Curtess Holmes (12)
The Meadows School, Coventry

Dragon

On a night so black, the thunder will crack.
This is his hunting call.
They track by the scent of smell so how can we tell
This is going to be a night of hell?

The shepherd knows this is the night;
A terrible nightmare will go to flight.
As the hours grow thin all the sheep fear for their skin.

The dragon's roar is as loud as thunder,
As from the sky it will come asunder.
First the shepherd sees the shadow so tall and big,
Then he hears the frightening call.

As he swoops down to take his prey,
He waits a second in delay.
Now the dragon strikes in rage
As if he has just been freed from a cage.

The sheep had no chance, its fate was sealed;
Only the blood was left in the field.
The dragon had performed his evil deed,
And now the shepherd must take more heed.

Bradley Gower (12)
The Meadows School, Coventry

The Bully

I wish I was the best, better than the rest.
I don't need to pass the test.
I rob your fags and I'll rob your money.
Give it to me or else I'll punch you in the tummy.
I think it's funny when you go crying to your mummy.
I'll make you laugh, I'll make you cry
And I will never say goodbye.

Gareth Sharman (12)
The Meadows School, Coventry

The Sniper

Sunday was my birthday
Damn it!
Smash!
The window shattered.

My mum came rushing in with my brother Tom,
Bang, bang!
A bullet straight through my mum's head.
Splat!
Blood came gushing out.
My brother Tom was screaming.
Bang!
A bullet straight into my stomach.
Bang!
My brother Tom is dead, he was only 6 months old.

My dad is a policeman.
He came in and said, 'Hey, honey, hey, honey, I'm home.'
Horror!
Everyone was dead
. . . Except me.

Dayle Wilson (13)
The Meadows School, Coventry

The New Butterfly

The butterfly is as colourful as the rainbow
And as nice as a rosy day.
Its wings are beautifully patterned
With red, green, blue and orange shapes.
The butterfly is as soft as a silken cloth.
Its wings are light as a rainbow and as dusty as icing sugar.
Its face a furry mask.
You can tell it is a butterfly
With its bright colours that can dazzle you.

Jack Hambridge (12)
The Meadows School, Coventry

A Poem About Homer Simpson

Homer is so lazy
All he does is
Watch TV and
Drink beer.

Homer is married to Marge
His son is called Bart
His daughters are Lisa and Maggie
His dog is called Santa's Little Helper
And all he does is watch TV and drink beer.

He works in the power plant
His boss' name is Mr Burns
At work he sits and eats doughnuts . . .

. . . And all he does is watch TV
And drink beer.
That is his life!

Seamus McGuire (14)
The Meadows School, Coventry

Dogs

They may be big,
They may be small,
I don't mind 'cause I love 'em all,
Long hair or short,
As long as it lasts,
My dog likes the bright green grass,
When I take him out he's always looking for a lass,
He barks and barks when someone walks past,
What about *your* dog?
What have *you* got?
'Cause I'm planning on buying the lot.
If they're big or even small,
I told you, I love them all.

Jamie Henderson (11)
The Meadows School, Coventry

Untitled

Bullies are bad
Their lives are sad
I don't think they like themselves
They make people's lives hell.

Sticks and stones may hurt my bones
But names will never hurt me

School life is hard
With bullies in the yard
They punch you, kick you hard
And hurt you.

Sticks and stones may hurt my bones
But names will never hurt me

It feels like
You're ready to die
Cry on the inside
Brave face outside.

Sticks and stones will hurt my bones
And names will *always* hurt me.

Luke Akers (12)
The Meadows School, Coventry

Drugs

Why do you want to hurt your body
With these terrible drugs?
When you've got some you act so smug
At the end of the day it's a waste
Of money, life and family
Why take this crap when you can get high naturally?
Why do you take speed and cocaine?
Please don't take the crap, it damages your brain
Can't you see what it's done to me?
Taking speed, cocaine and LSD
Eventually it will ruin your life
You could die, think of your family
These drugs are pain
They say no pain, no gain
I think it's a load of crap all the same
You think you're a gangster, you act so hard
When actually, you'll soon need a death card
Drugs are bad, they'll harm you and your family

Why do you do it?

Jack Connell (13)
The Meadows School, Coventry

A Visit To The Zoo

I went to the zoo and had something to eat
And the zoo animals ate the food
They are so bad
Why do they have to eat the food?
They will get fat and fat
So stop eating the food and you will be happy
And everyone will like you
So will you stop eating the food?
I have to go now so bye and have a good time at the zoo
I have to go to my nan's
Bye, I will see you again
Bye for now
I will bring you some food next time
I will bring you your favourite
I will
I promise
You can count on me
Bye, everyone
I will see you next time when I next come to the zoo
I had a good time
It was the best time in my life
I wish I could have you for a pet
But you are bit big to fit in my house
I will visit you again
I promise
I have to go now
Bye.

Chris Clarke (13)
The Meadows School, Coventry

Drugs

You're a smack head, crack head
The lowest of the low
Flies follow you around wherever you go
You never got the highs
Always the lows
Steal money from people you're close to
Drugs - a waste
Have no taste
They don't have a place in the human race

Some people take weed and speed
Some people take cocaine
Just messes up their brains to reveal their pain
They get a buzz like a bumblebee by taking Es
LSD - it disgusts me
But it's not as bad as Ecstasy
It messes up the family and those that are close to me

They always look out of their head
They should stay in bed
It makes them see red and get mad
Caught by the local Fed - his name is Ted

One thing leads to another
Drugs, a life of crime
Think of your brother and others
It's a loser's game
It is such a shame

Make something out of life!

Shay Oliver (14)
The Meadows School, Coventry

Racism

I hate racism
It's like a foul taste in my mouth
It doesn't matter if you're from north, east, west or south.
Its smell smacks you in the face
Even though you are the other side of town.

I hate racism
It's like your heart and soul being swallowed up
Into a big, black hole.
Out of the souls there is always one
Has to spoil the fun.

I hate racism
It's always aimed on black
And some white
Trying to make a living in the UK and the USA
Even guys hate blacks and white some days.

I hate racism
I hate the sound of the word
They should let it burn
Let the whole world know how much it really hurts
So just let it burn.

Jamie Worwood (15)
The Meadows School, Coventry

French Troops Resting

Men, men, a load of men,
Sitting at their roadside den,
Sitting, sleeping, waiting till when,
They get the call of attack again.

Guns, guns, a load of guns,
Sitting, lying on their buns,
Waiting till they see the sun,
Then their day has just begun.

Bergans, bergans, a load of bergans,
Here come the lights searchen, searchen,
It's the alarm sounden, sounden,
Here come the Germans, runnin', runnin'.

Bodies dying, bodies dying, a load of bodies dying,
Being shot dead, they're all crying,
A bullet just missed me, *whew* in sighing,
Argh! I've just been shot, now I'm dying.

I'm dying, I'm dying, a load of dying,
Here, mate, take my wedding ring,
Take it back to my French darling,
Take it to her, tell her I love her but I'm dying.

Philip Ball (15)
The Meadows School, Coventry

Prison

If my brother hadn't have assaulted someone
He wouldn't have to go to jail,
And I wouldn't have had to see him try and get bail.
Sometimes I sit alone at night wondering if my poor bro is alright.

I wonder how he feels sitting in a cell,
If I was him I'd feel like I was in Hell.
All he's got is a smelly, old bed,
I wonder what is going through his head.

Every night I hear my mum saying she is very sad,
Even though what he did is pretty bad.
I can see her heart is broken,
Every day she waits for the postman
For news of my brother.
Every day is another yesterday.

I went to see him, he looks like a different human being,
His face is proper gloomy,
His cell is so doomy.
Apparently last night he had a massive fight,
The next time I see him -
God help him be alright.

Josh Nagle (12)
The Meadows School, Coventry

Cars

Cars, cars,
Modified cars,
Some with full body kits,
Some with some fancy bits.
My favourite car is an Evo 8,
In this car I'll never be late.
It looks kind of slick
And I know it is very quick!

Adam Johnson (12)
The Meadows School, Coventry

Don't Lose It!

This is my life
Stay low, lay low, don't show
Sit alone and I cry and I'd rather die
Don't throw a punch - throw lunch.

Don't lose your temper
Just remember
Don't lose it
Listen to music
Nobody gonna encrypt my script
Everything I own.
Gonna make it on my own
But I'm all alone
Once I go over these tracks
I'm never gonna look back.

Suddenly a new burst of energy has occurred
But it's everything to me 'cause it's my creditability
Sometimes I think my life ain't worth livin'
Because I'm always trippin'
No more games
I'm in a cold rage
But the mood has all changed.

Jamie Braithwaite (14)
The Meadows School, Coventry

Evening After A Push

The tree that no longer has life,
Its branches splintered and charred,
Its only company dead, rotting soldiers.

Men in uniform holding their guns,
Their heads hung in sadness and despair,
In no-man's-land.

The sky seems dull,
Except for the light that is searching,
Searching for enemy planes.

In the distance a ray of light,
Only just visible through the clouds,
This light is the only hope for the soldiers -
In no-man's-land.

Matthew Griffiths (14)
The Meadows School, Coventry

The Attic!

Up in the loft
Where it's darker
Than dark,
It's getting quite cold
So I tremble and
Shiver,
I hear a strange
Sound, so I
Panic and run,
To turn on the light,
That's the end of the
Fun!

Claire Waring (12)
The Nottingham Emmanuel School, Nottingham

Do You Believe?

Do you believe there's anything up there?
Do you believe, up there in the sky?

Do you believe in limitless joy?
Do you believe in angels that fly?

Do you believe that we go somewhere different?
Do you believe we go when we die?

Do you believe in devilish sin?
Do you believe a sin is to cry?

Do you believe there's anything up there?
Do you believe, as do I?

Do you see the world different?
Do you believe?
Do you believe?

Tom Mason (12)
The Nottingham Emmanuel School, Nottingham

Mirror, Mirror

Mirror, mirror, on the wall,
I am more hideous than them all.
I don't think I can take much more,
Was Miss Popular telling the truth?
I'm not sure.
Maybe I should diet,
I'll wash my greasy hair tonight,
There's that boy I fancy,
If I want him, I'll have to fight.
On my face I have so many spots,
My face is going red, but I just can't stop.
I'm frustrated, I'm crying, I just can't think,
I need to calm down or else I'll sink.
Mirror, mirror, on the wall,
Please let me be more beautiful than them all.

Daniella Binch (13)
The Nottingham Emmanuel School, Nottingham

Victim

I groan and clutch my stomach,
But the pain is in my heart.
Say I don't feel well,
I don't,
I think.
I can't go to school,
I don't look right,
Don't think right,
Don't act right.
I'm afraid,
Afraid of life,
Afraid,
Afraid of myself,
Afraid,
Afraid of them,
Afraid,
Just afraid.

Seonaid Beaumont (12)
The Nottingham Emmanuel School, Nottingham

I Love You

I love you, I love you
I wish you really knew
My passion, my love
But you'll probably never know
But you go off with another boy
I can't bear it, I can't
I wish you had the same love for me
As you do for him
My tears, my tears, they're about to brim.

Luke Derby (13)
The Nottingham Emmanuel School, Nottingham

I Feel People Watching Me

I feel people watching me
Danger lurks on each street corner
I'm a renegade for all to see
Either they're growing shorter or I'm growing taller

Somebody grabs my arm
I shout and I bite and I scream
I run all the way home to safety
And hide away from harm

Somebody knocks at the door
He's got a gun
I run and run
Until I can't run anymore

Just because I'm paranoid doesn't mean they're not out to get me.

Does it?

Jamie Buchan (13)
The Nottingham Emmanuel School, Nottingham

Evolution

A small, pathetic, insignificant being,
To become the world we live in.

To form the creatures of this Earth
And to give this planet its modern worth.

It will grow and grow and multiply,
Be born, grow up and then must die.

It will adapt through subtle changes,
In this world and its many ages.

It will develop into individual types
And each will lead separate lives.

It will evolve, develop and
Will live in each and every land.

Rory Devonport (13)
The Nottingham Emmanuel School, Nottingham

Skipping A Beat

When you're in love,
Your heart skips a beat,
Butterflies floating above,
From your head to your feet.

You make an effort to look sweet,
You rush your tea, lunch or dinner,
You make your hair perfect and neat,
You go out thinking you're a winner.

Then reality hits you,
Your heart no longer skips a beat,
You realise you're no longer the awesome two,
There's now only one pair of feet.

You're all alone,
You're just a one-man band,
Clutching hold of your phone,
Wanting someone to understand.

Emma Upton (13)
The Nottingham Emmanuel School, Nottingham

Unconsciousness

What happens when you are unconscious?
No one really knows.
You're strolling along then a knock on the head.
Everything just goes.

You see nothing, feel nothing.
You're completely oblivious.
Unfeeling, unknowing,
In a hollow emptiness.

When you're unconscious you can see a bright light ahead,
Is what some people say.
Which are in fact the gates of Heaven,
Welcoming you to stay.

But what I think is that the time just flies.
You go unconscious but you can't really tell.
You don't think, you don't remember,
Then in an instant wake up where you fell.

Simon Verhoeven (12)
The Nottingham Emmanuel School, Nottingham

Writing Competition

I saw the words on the blackboard
Writing competition
What could I do?
A story, a stanza, a sonnet
No, no, no!
I sat there thinking
Thinking
Thinking
I jerked out of my reverie
A voice barking, 'Half an hour left'
What could I do?
I suddenly desperately started to write
I wrote faster than light
Lines, verses, pages, all flowing from my pen
I wou- *'Time up!'* shouted the teacher
I sat, numb with shock
As we walked out I reflected
It was only a poem anyway . . .

Chris Ford
The Nottingham Emmanuel School, Nottingham

Fears

Lying in bed, fears spinning round like a whirlwind in my head.
Crash, clatter, creak! What was that?
Wild imaginings fill my head,
Monsters creeping round my bed.

Pulse races,
Heart chases,
Breath flies away.

Door squeaks,
Floor creaks,
Wind whistles through the house.

In the darkness I can see a strange creature walking towards me.
Up it jumps on my bed and walks right over to my head.
It licks my face as gentle as can be.

The creature that brought terror to my house,
Now seems like a timid mouse.
Snuggles up, fears flee, soon we're sleeping happily.

Lois Brown (13)
The Nottingham Emmanuel School, Nottingham

Spiders Everywhere

Why are we afraid of them?
They're only tiny,
But to us,
Spiders are like big, black holes
Swirling into the darkness,
The darkness.
Screaming when you're dreaming
Of spiders,
Nightmares,
They're just nightmares.
Spiders come in different shapes and sizes,
But,
We're still frightened.
Why?
We just are.
Spiders are everywhere,
No matter what you do,
They're still there.
It's hard, I know that,
You know that,
We know that.
It's hard to overcome your fear,
Spiders are everywhere
And always will be.

Kelly Ridley (12)
The Nottingham Emmanuel School, Nottingham

What Is Going To Happen Now?

I am unconscious
I am going to die
I need to remember.

Music is part of my life
But now I hear no music
Now I am fading away

For good.

I am scared of everything
Not just death
Spiders, heights, the dark

My heartbeat's getting quicker
Is that good?

Death is resounding through my head
Will my olive green eyes ever see the light again?
Green for go
Where am I going now?

I must not stop
I need to remember
Wait, what's this?
Why can I see light?
I still have a heartbeat
I am in hospital

I am alive.

Emma Boulton (13)
The Nottingham Emmanuel School, Nottingham

Unconsciousness

Engulfed by a world of mild grey
Being rolled along the ground
You scream but there's no sound coming out
You finally stop after what seems like hours
And stop your silent scream

You stand and look around you
Nothing to see but grey
You decide to rejoin the world you know
You run back the way you rolled from
But nothing is coming near

As you continue along your self-made road
A dark spot catches your eye
You turn around and face it
Dark coils entwine around your body
You start to feel suffocated
But still fail to make a sound

You sit around and wonder
What you did to deserve this
When you see a bright light
Looking warm and firm and safe

The light is getting nearer
That's something you can clearly see
You step inside the soothing field
Only to feel your eyes ablaze
You find your friends around you; you're lying on the floor
'You'll never guess where I've been,' you say . . .
And you're right, they never do!

Daniel Flint (13)
The Nottingham Emmanuel School, Nottingham

The Knight And The Dragon

As the keep comes into view
The knight settles down to rest
He draws his sword for protection
And sings aloud with zest

For tomorrow the knight will slay
The one beast he is yet to test
The mighty dragon in its keep
To prove which beast is best

Although the rest was needed
The knight had a troubled sleep
Having visions of himself
Alone in the dragon's keep

And so the knight awakes blurrily
And reaches for the sword, but soon
He packs up the camp and leaves
Ready for the fight to come

As he enters the keep
He has his sword in one hand, and his pride in the other
He charges at the dragon, sword raised
And pierces it from behind

The dragon teeters with anger
The knight backs away
And all he could say is:
'Die beast!' his voice full of violence and power

And so the knight leaves the keep
Proud and joyful
Onto the future road
To find what he'll slay.

Daniel Neville (13)
The Nottingham Emmanuel School, Nottingham

Necrophobia

It shivers my bones
It shatters my heart
It makes my blood run cold
Necrophobia

It keeps my mind going
It freezes my tongue
It sickens my stomach
Necrophobia

It whispers in my ear
It silences my mouth
It blinds my eyes
Necrophobia.

It curses my brain
It chatters my teeth
It makes my life history
Necrophobia.

George Gadd (13)
The Nottingham Emmanuel School, Nottingham

The Unknown

The unknown . . . that's its name,
The desolate forest with no sound
Apart from the rippling of the water,
The scurrying of the rodents
And the gust of wind blowing from time to time.
The snow-capped trees blow in the bitter winter air,
While the stars wink persistently,
Like tiny grains of glitter against a chalkboard.
The moon shimmers like foil,
Reflecting onto the lake with a thin layer of frost.

The bats flap their wings innocently,
Flying smoothly among the darkness.
The owls hoot constantly,
Whilst perched on the fragile branches,
Almost as if they are waiting for a hoot in reply.
From whom? Who knows?

The smell of moss surrounds the lonesome atmosphere,
The dried up leaves crunch as little mice scamper
Swiftly across the land.
The wild cry of wolves sound violently
Through the evening breeze.

Ellis Dunkley (13)
The Nottingham Emmanuel School, Nottingham

Fear

Fear
Skulks in the shadows . . . waiting.
Fear
Follows behind, just out of reach.
Fear
Makes sounds, scaring my soul.
Fear
Gnaws at the back of my mind.
Fear
Outwits even the calmest kind.
Fear
Tenses when you hesitate.
Fear
Springs when you doubt.
Fear
Grips you like a vice.
Fear
When it's got you, the lights go out.

Matt Slater (13)
The Nottingham Emmanuel School, Nottingham

Animal Parade

I went to Woburn Abbey
And saw an elephant there
He gave me a set of keys
But I only came up to his knees.

I went to Woburn Abbey
And saw a lion there
He gave a mighty roar
It gave me a bit of a scare!

I went to Woburn Abbey
And saw a zebra there
His stripes were black, his skin was white
It needs a lot of care!

Cara Neale
The Ralph Sadleir School, Puckeridge

Celebrate A Friend

I want to be friends with you
Till the Earth goes flat
And the grass turns purple

If we are friends
I'll let you borrow my make-up
Let you be first in line
And I'll share my snacks with you

I will give you
My favourite pair of shoes
My last piece of chocolate
And my favourite gel pen

I will like you more than Friday afternoons
My favourite magazine
And my Simms computer game
You will be my best friend.

Charlotte Marro (11)
The Ralph Sadleir School, Puckeridge

Hectic Classroom

Break time finishes, in the classroom,
Lots of noise and plenty of movement,
No teacher here,
So there are people shouting and complaining,
Running around making an earthquake,
Desks rattling, chairs moving,
Sounds like fingers on a blackboard.
Then suddenly, 'Teacher's coming,' is called.
Everything stops, everything's quiet,
People sit down reading books.
Teacher comes in, 'Well done,' he says.
If only he knew what had really been happening,
I'd be doomed!

Amy Carter (11)
The Ralph Sadleir School, Puckeridge

River, River

River, river,
Wherever you go,
River, river,
You will flow.

River, river,
In the hill,
River, river,
You will flow through all the mills.

River, river,
In the ground,
Turning, turning,
Going round.

River, river,
Wherever you go,
River, river,
You will always flow.

George Cook (11)
The Ralph Sadleir School, Puckeridge

Promise Of Friendship

I want to be friends with you until:
The world turns upside down
The dodos come back to life
The buses can walk.

If we are friends I will:
Let you walk my dog
Let you ride my bike
Let you bake some cakes.

I will give you:
A share of my chocolate
All of my money
My silver flip-up phone.

Becky Bird (11)
The Ralph Sadleir School, Puckeridge

Promise Of Friendship

I want to be friends with you
Until snails have legs
And can go faster than running pigs,
The Simpsons come to life,
The great roaring sea is empty
And the fluffy cotton clouds fall out of the sky.

I will give you:
The gold at the end of the rainbow,
The bigger part of a chocolate cake
And the shine of the sun.

If we are friends I will:
Pick you up when you're down,
Give you money when you're skint
And give you my best jewellery.

I will like you more than:
A day out shopping at Lakeside,
The way the sun beams on the ground
And blue Smarties.

Chloe Fox (11)
The Ralph Sadleir School, Puckeridge

Monkey Business

The monkey swings from tree to tree
Way too high for you and me
It travels quickly through the air
It moves like there's no time to spare.

It has two hands and owns two feet
Leaves and sticks are what it eats
Monkeys act like us sometimes
You will see if you read between the lines.

Heather Gillam
The Ralph Sadleir School, Puckeridge

The River

The river
    Runs
    Just
    Like
 A
Snake,
  It
    Sits
      There
 Just
Like
      It's awake.
            I
        Stand
        And
Stare
      Just over
            There,
            Near
            The
            Wall.
  I
        Really
            Hope
        I
        Don't
Fall.

Jourdana Fairlie (11)
The Ralph Sadleir School, Puckeridge

River

The river flows through the valley,
Streams join river, river flows on,
Round a bend, down a hill, off to the sea,
Past a weeping willow tree.

James Backham (11)
The Ralph Sadleir School, Puckeridge

Celebrate A Friend

I want to be friends with you
Until the whole world splits in half
And the sun and the moon
Melt and turn green.

If we are friends
I will let you have a bit of my snack
And I would also let you have
The last chicken fan at lunch
Even though I love chicken fans.

I will give you all my jewellery
You can also borrow my DVDs
You can have lots of my shoes.

I like you more
Than my big cuddly teddy
And also my CDs
And my beautiful rabbits.

Natasha Mead
The Ralph Sadleir School, Puckeridge

Fireworks

Catherine wheels go round and round,
Rockets shoot up from the ground,
Sparklers spit out a crackling sound,
Animals safe at home.

Golden rain shatters like glass,
Eyes are gleaming as they pass,
Just the empties left on the grass,
Found tomorrow when all is quiet.

Josh Davies (11)
The Ralph Sadleir School, Puckeridge

Fireworks

Crash! Bang! Goes the screamer
As it soars through the air,
And all of the animals
Going into despair.

The fire is crackling
And the sparklers are bright,
Dad is busy
Setting the fireworks alight.

The rockets are screeching
And the people are in a line,
Mum is in the kitchen
Drinking all of the wine.

The candles are glowing
And the firework box is bare,
All I can smell
Is smoke in the air.

Nanny is hungry
It's not a pretty sight,
So just beware
She can give you a bite.

The food is ready
And Mum is very giddy,
Dad won't come in
Because he's acting like a kiddie.

The food is finished
I know Dad will appear,
He will say goodnight
As the people disappear.

While I am in bed
Dad will have beer,
But just remember the mayhem
Is only once a year.

Sam Deville (11)
The Ralph Sadleir School, Puckeridge

Promise Of Friendship

I want to be friends with you until:
The leaves turn blue,
Buses can walk
And the ocean is dry.

I will give you:
My last piece of chocolate,
The key to the clouds
And the warmth of the sun on my face.

If we are friends I will:
Lend you my special pen
And I will lend you
My glittery lipgloss.

I like you more than:
My fluffy teddy bear,
And the cold, cuddly snow
In my back garden.

Georgia Higgins (11)
The Ralph Sadleir School, Puckeridge

A Promise Of Friendship

I want to be friends with you until the sun dies
And when all the water has run out
And till I stop loving my mum.

If we were friends I would let you borrow my favourite pen
And I would buy you a break if you don't have one.
I'd let you choose which bunk you want to sleep in
If I have a sleepover.

I will give you my favourite keyring
And I will let you cuddle my favourite toy dog.

I like you more than all the animals in the world
And purple Smarties.

I will be your best friend!

Robyn Turner
The Ralph Sadleir School, Puckeridge

Promise Of Friendship

I want to be friends with you until
My dog turns pink
The world bounces out of the universe
The grandfather clock strikes thirteen.

If we are friends I will
Give you a make-over
Teach you how to ride a quad bike
Take you to see a famous person
I will give you
The fitness of PE
My last Rolo
The moon.

I will like you more than
A pack of Mars Delight
My favourite teddy bears
My annoying little sister.

Aimée Jeromson (11)
The Ralph Sadleir School, Puckeridge

River Poem

We set off at half-past nine,
Ready with our boots,
The teacher said we mustn't whine,
While tripping over tree roots.

Giggles, laughter and lots of talking,
Got us excited but we kept on walking.
Having fun while learning,
Listening to the river churning.
Through the Lordship on our way,
Thinking that we had to stay.
On the way back I talked to my mate,
Thank goodness we weren't late.
We got home ready for lunch,
I couldn't wait to have a munch.

Kate Davies
The Ralph Sadleir School, Puckeridge

Young Writers - Great Minds From Near And Far

Promise Of Friendship

I want to be friends with you until:
The last of the sun is seen
The sky turns pink
And money grows on trees.

If we are friends I will:
Lend you my 100cm ruler
Let you have the first swim in my pool
And the first bite of my Galaxy bar.

I will give you:
The blade of ice from last Christmas
The gold from the first leaf in autumn
And the colour of tulips in spring.

I will like you more than:
The first day of summer
The presents on Christmas Day
And my favourite designer outfit.

Eveigh Noble (11)
The Ralph Sadleir School, Puckeridge

A River Poem

R unning down the pasture fields,
 I n the river silt is made,
V ery pretty as it flows,
E verlasting,
R iver, river, stay with me

F lowing softly in the wind,
L ovely flowers round the banks,
O ver the hills it flushes by,
W ater gushes,
 I n the wind,
N ever stopping,
G oing to the sea.

Sara Gilbert (11)
The Ralph Sadleir School, Puckeridge

River

The river flows,
The sky shows,
In its snaking banks.
It gleams and thanks the sun,
For her reflection,
Conscious of her looks.

The river glows,
In the midnight sun,
In its snaking banks.
It shines with translucent glory,
The reeds sway with the flowing current,
Through the eroded banks.

The ducks and flitting fish
In the nearby reeds,
Wake the morning
As the old man walks his dog.

Lana Premadasa
The Ralph Sadleir School, Puckeridge

My Favourite Fireworks

My favourite fireworks shimmer in the dark,
If my dogs see them they will bark.

My favourite fireworks pop and sizzle,
They make a big noise even if they're little.

My favourite fireworks are the rockets,
But they could take your arms out of their sockets.

My favourite fireworks look like glitter in the sky,
I could easily watch them all night.

Bianca Burridge (11)
The Ralph Sadleir School, Puckeridge

Literacy Lesson Gone Wrong

Children file in,
Sit down, then . . .
Havoc!
Paper planes zoom across the room.
Teacher yells,
'Put that down,
Don't throw that,
Calm down, stop it,
Ouch!'
Children not listening, teacher yelling,
Head teacher walks in and
Children scramble back to their seats.
Teacher about to throw plane back, then . . .
'What on earth are you doing?'
Teacher looks ashamed.
'They made me do it,' she squeaked.
Children giggle,
Head teacher looks angry.
'Alright, back to the staffroom with you.'
Stares at class,
'And while you're there, tell Miss Vast
Class 5B needs you.'
Children gulp, classroom silent.

Charlotte Kearley (11)
The Ralph Sadleir School, Puckeridge

Tiger

I saw a tiger in the grass,
Waiting for an antelope to pass.
His plan was to run and leap,
But when the antelope arrived . . .
He was asleep.

Oliver Kerr (11)
The Ralph Sadleir School, Puckeridge

Promise Of Friendship

I want to be friends with you until:
The first man lands on Mars,
Until the leaves of a tree turn blue
And until someone lives to be 1,000 years old.

I will like you more than:
The warmth of the golden sun,
The soft powdery smell of my mum
And the metallic shine of the moon.

If we are friends I will:
Be your partner all the time,
Let you borrow my favourite teddy
And give you the cherry on top of my cake.

I will give you:
The sweetness of honey and sugar,
The colours of the rainbow
And the cotton of the clouds.

Catherine Sheridan (11)
The Ralph Sadleir School, Puckeridge

The River

R ivers we need
 I nching towards the sea
V eering side to side
E nding only at the sea
R iver, river, don't leave me

F lowing like a leaf in a breeze
L ong and winding is the river
O tters jumping in and out
W inding down and down
 I nviting and cool
N aughty currents washing the shore
G oing to the sea.

Peter Dalton (11)
The Ralph Sadleir School, Puckeridge

Promise Of Friendship

I want to be friends with you until:
My dog turns pink,
The world bounces
And the grandfather clock strikes thirteen.

If we are friends I will let you:
Ride my purple and pink bike,
Borrow my denim coat and my teddy bear,
Give you the fitness of PE,
My last Rolo
And my annoying little sister.

I will like you more than:
The sweetness of chocolate,
A lemon sherbet sweet
And the joy of Christmas.

Sarah Jackson (11)
The Ralph Sadleir School, Puckeridge

Promise Of Friendship

I want to be friends with you until:
Time stops in its tracks,
All volcanoes erupt,
The sun dies and turns into a black hole.

If we are friends I will:
Let you use my ideas
And eat my slice of chocolate cake at lunch,
I will pass the ball to you in footie.

I will give you:
The wind in the trees,
The pot of gold behind the rainbow
And the smell of newly washed clothes.

I will like you more than:
White, fluffy snow on winter days,
The orange glowing sun beating down on the Earth.

Robert England (11)
The Ralph Sadleir School, Puckeridge

Celebrate A Friend

I want to be friends with you until:
The Earth is empty,
Until the moon has disappeared,
Until the sun has turned to ice.

If we are friends I will:
Lend you my best straightener,
I will lend you my teddy bear,
I will lend you my other folder for school.

I will give you:
My other bike,
My other half of my best friend necklace
And the other half of my snack.

I will like you more than:
My favourite pencil case,
My favourite sweets
And more than my favourite TV show.

Shauni Barrett (11)
The Ralph Sadleir School, Puckeridge

What Is Green?

Green is a slithery snake in your garden
Green is a Brussels sprout that's on your plate
Green is a car zooming along the road
And green is a green bike and the Hulk.

Green is a green tropical bird flying
Green is a grasshopper in a trap
Green is a pea rolling on your plate
And a crocodile in the lake.

Green is a person being sick
Green is a lizard in a cage
Green is a motorbike before going on jumps
And green is Tango and green Twisters.

Steven Fredericks (11)
The Ralph Sadleir School, Puckeridge

As Black As Death

As black as death,
As black as a witch's cat,
As black as a flapping bat,
As black as the midnight sky,
As black as the coal on a fire,
As black as a rain-filled cloud,
As black as a sulking goth,
As black as space,
As black as a killer whale's back.

Charlotte Williams (11)
The Ralph Sadleir School, Puckeridge

Untitled

Blue as the dark, dangerous ocean,
As blue as the bright blue sky,
As blue as the crashing ocean waves,
As blue as the sparkling wide ocean,
As blue as a deep blue sapphire,
As blue as the Caribbean Ocean.

Thomas Santurri (11)
The Ralph Sadleir School, Puckeridge

Fireworks

When I see fireworks
Zoom into the sky
If they don't make a boom
I give a big sigh.

Red ones
Yellow ones
Orange and blue
Catherine wheels and sparklers too.

Rufus Pratt
The Ralph Sadleir School, Puckeridge

Promise Of Friendship

I want to be friends with you until:
We are ten feet tall,
The stars fall out of the sky
And the clouds turn to candyfloss.

I will give you:
The glowing colours of the rainbow,
All the dazzling beauty of the peacock
And my last red jelly baby.

If we are friends I will:
Let you choose the popcorn at the cinema
And tell you my embarrassing secrets.

I will like you more than:
The silvery moon on a starlit night,
Tiny, spotted ladybirds
And skyscraper heels.

Jasmin Geddes-Rainbow (11)
The Ralph Sadleir School, Puckeridge

Untitled

Emerald as a green traffic light
Emerald as green as the green in the rainbow
Emerald as the long grass
Emerald as a newborn leaf
Emerald as the bushes in a garden
Emerald as neatly cut out hedges
Emerald as the mould on rocks
Emerald as a shiny birthstone ring
Emerald as the sparkly seas
Emerald as a sparkling lizard.

Gillian Gibbons (11)
The Ralph Sadleir School, Puckeridge

The Ostrich

The ostrich plodded round his plot
And hung his head in boredom.
Oh, to be a bird that flies
Across the big blue sky!

He soared over the sea like a black-backed gull,
Glided like a shearwater
And dived into the deep blue ocean
Like a gannet.

He undulated like a mistle thrush,
Zoomed through the air like a swallow
And carved the trees like a woodpecker.

He rose in the hot air like a buzzard,
Hovered high like a kestrel
And stooped suddenly like a peregrine.

Then landed with a bump on the floor of his plot.

Tom Jeffries (11)
The Ralph Sadleir School, Puckeridge

Wood Brown

As brown as a leafless forest,
As brown as a summer wood,
As brown as an old oak tree,
As brown as wood can be,
As brown as an old antique.

As brown as the bark on a tree,
As brown as a forest of trees,
As brown as the trunk of a tree
And as brown as an old dock near the sea.

James Danter (11)
The Ralph Sadleir School, Puckeridge

Memories Of Primary School

You linger in the doorway
While the teacher welcomes you in
You play and run around like scavenging ants
Making new friends.
You learn the alphabet
Days of the week
Months of the year
Chanting each one
So it remains in your memory for evermore.

Second after second
Minute after minute
Hour after hour goes by like a flash of light,
One day merging into the next.
You start to feel like you're in a time machine,
Every year goes by so quickly.
Same lessons every day,
Same people,
Same journey . . .

Then a bell like a siren rings!
Time for fun!
No time for work!
You're It!
No, you are!

You get back to your lesson, refreshed,
To the musty smell of your teacher's perfume,
To the display of young artists like an art gallery.
A drawer each with your name on it.
You could put what you want in there,
It was yours!

The incessant talking of young people,
Like birds at daybreak,
Unable to concentrate on their work.
Watching older children outside
Through the one-way windows,
So you could see them, but they couldn't see you.

The end of the day.
Your mum comes to pick you up.
She asks how your day's been.
You shrug your shoulders, impatient to get home,
To watch TV,
To play in the park,
To do anything but wait around for one more second.

Holidays come and at last you're free!
Free to explore and do whatever you want!
But you are glad to get back to school with your friends.
Even though it's hard,
You realise you're another year older.
One year closer to leaving.
One year closer to having no rules.

Catherine Keene (13)
Tottington High School, Bury

A Monkey Called Ross

The animals suffer alone, in silence they lay,
As the world gets polluted day by day,
The trees fall to the ground with a loud thud,
Water has evaporated, leaving just mud,
Lions, tigers, birds and bears,
Are left alone, alone and scared,
This is because they have no home,
Left alone, alone, alone.
Sat in a little pile of moss,
Sits a small baby monkey called Ross,
His siblings, mum and dad have died,
So baby Ross just sits and cries,
Ross has no home, no family left,
He sits and cries, he is bereft,
This is because of pollution,
Yet there always is a better solution.

Katie Eves (13)
Tottington High School, Bury

A School Day

The sun came up,
The day began,
At a quarter to nine,
Little children and their mums,
Walked up the dull, grey pavement.
They looked as if they were in a trance.

In the ring of a bell,
The children vanished
Like a crowd at a football match.
Singing daily became a chore,
Sometimes it was quite a bore.
Another bell, lessons began.

Classrooms smelling clean and fresh,
Chairs placed neatly on the desk.
The children listened intently,
Fixed, like they were hypnotized.
A working silence filled the air,
Minds ticking, pens scribbling.
Far away you could hear Mrs Law preaching
Like an MP on the television.

Another shrill bell broke the silence.
In an instant, people were hurrying out to play.
The noise was like standing in the Kop,
All standing, all swaying, all crushed.

Children running around,
Squealing, shouting, arguing,
Eating crisps, devouring food
Like a vacuum cleaner sucking up dust.

It came to the afternoon,
Each child looking at the clock,
Longing to go home.
Seconds became minutes,
Minutes became hours,
Time was going as slow as watching a plant grow.

A sudden outbreak of life,
Games.
The four houses - Holcombe, Pendle, Rivington, Knowel,
Racing against each other.
The atmosphere became electric.
Dashes of colour flashing before their eyes,
The ear-piercing sound of whistle shook the air.

Getting back into uniform,
Rushing like there was no tomorrow,
Trying to sneak out before the bell,
The wooden door laughed as they tried but couldn't open it.

5, 4, 3, 2, 1,
The last bell rang.
It felt like a lifetime had gone by.
A wave of children flooded the streets.
Freedom.

Lea Taylor (13)
Tottington High School, Bury

Lowercroft Memories

The bell rang.
The summer holidays had finished.
You stepped into school
With your uniform as red as a sunset.

Mr Lansdale was strict and funny.
Mrs Law was religious and forgetful.
Mr Mellor was old, but loved maths, so he was no dummy.
Mrs Cliffe was grey and fretful.

I remember trapping a dinner lady's hand in the door.
I remember a tile falling on Charlie's head.
I remember Thursday's assembly, what a bore!
Nevertheless, it had to be said,
'Lowercroft days were the best!'

Sam Winstanley (13)
Tottington High School, Bury

The Environment

Blue bins, black bins, brown bins galore,
Don't drop your litter on the floor,
Recycle your litter,
Protect the Earth,
Prevent pollution,
For what it's worth.

Global warming
And climate change,
Is like the overwhelming heat
Of a fire burning page.

Coal, oil and gas,
Pollute the air,
They are non-renewable,
So we must take care.

Asthma sufferers,
Gradually increasing,
As different gases
Mix together.

A grey cloud of poison
Lies in the sky,
Dramatically changing the weather.

Recycling and *thinking*
Makes the air much cleaner,
We are saving the environment,
Now that people are a lot keener.

The environment is always changing,
For the good or for the bad,
What can you do to help?
A lot!
Not just *a tad!*

Annabelle Kelly (13)
Tottington High School, Bury

My Personal Little Memories Of Primary

When you walked in there was
A smile like the sun,
Or a frown like there was no tomorrow,
She had her good days and bad,
But was she happy or sad?

'Be good and I'll be good to you,'
Is what she used to say.
She never forgot that phrase,
Like a baby never leaves its bottle,
That was our teacher, Miss Cottle.

Our silly playground games,
Like silly was just stupid,
We never stopped to think,
Like a baby never stops the cries,
They were our silly playground times.

The bald-headed master,
It was as if hair couldn't grow,
He stayed sat in his room,
Like a prisoner sat in their cell,
The only time he left was at the lunch bell.

Our neat little secretary,
Who was always happy to help,
She was like Carol Vordeman,
She would always be on the ball,
You could not fault her at all.

Those were my little memories of primary,
Smells of antiseptic when we fell,
Sights of children when they draw,
Tastes of cold, thin gravy,
It feels like I'm back at my primary.

Melissa Butterworth (13)
Tottington High School, Bury

A Mature Infant Year

A new beginning, a new chapter of your life,
Still an infant, yet you feel much more mature,
Your heart aches with the excitement, the anticipation,
As it leaps like a leopard on the prowl.
You're walking, you're closer, closer to that room,
It glows like Heaven and welcomes you happily.
Bright, vibrant colours, like a play centre,
So enthralling, tantalizing, you must go in.

You enter, palms perspiring with nerves,
Looking around at your friends, all terrified of what's to come,
Is she nice? Strict? You don't know.
Shaking like a leaf, you take a seat,
The suspense cutting into you like a painful blade,
That well known sinking lump in your throat
And she enters, the teacher.

Like your guardian angel, Miss Allsop,
She is caring, kind.
A sweet, soft voice, like melting caramel,
You hang on every word, thirst for such knowledge.
You sit with your best friend and the two strange boys
And play with the maps, sharks leaping at you from the sea.

You felt so safe, overwhelmed by the school, your castle,
With tall, strong, protecting walls,
That lovely, yet strange aroma of wax crayons that
Stays with you for the rest of your life.

Suddenly, the atmosphere is tense,
Your walls are breaking down,
A word is hissed down the room,
A word. You don't know its meaning,
But it terrifies you more than the monster under the bed.

Now, you're sitting at a desk,
Those moist palms are back, as is the lump in your throat
And there is a deathly silence, swirling.
You answer the interrogation, the questions,
Shuddering as you worry if you've answered correctly.
When it's over, you're dragged out by a cheering crowd.
It's over, the SATs.

Now it's time for childish games,
Like 'witches' or 'tig',
Those games you never tire of.
And as you run, you feel
A sense of pride
As now, you begin your next chapter, the next moment,
The next year.

Gabriella Sloss (13)
Tottington High School, Bury

Save Our World

The trees whisper,
As the wind blows,
Spring has just begun,
Flowers start to grow.

But then people come along
And then litter hits the ground.
The smoke puffs out,
Pollution all around.

Factories, industries,
Polluting the air,
Global warming, waste management,
Nobody seems to care.

New forms of energy,
We will have to use,
Because the fossil fuels,
We are about to lose.

People are now starting to realise,
How we are destroying the world,
We must do something before it's too late,
Changing our ways to *save our world!*

Victoria Hinde (13)
Tottington High School, Bury

Year 4

Year 4 was the worst year of my life.
We had a new teacher called Mrs Coogan.
Her voice was like a drowning cat
And she droned on and on like a broken record
Until I fell asleep,
Then I was woken up by a screaming banshee.

First it was boring numeracy,
With the cheap books and easy questions.
Then the bell went
And everyone ran outside happy and screaming.
It was Monday, toast day,
Or more like 5-year old toast that's cold toast day
And the usual war between us and the Year 3's.
We have been doing this forever.

After break it's CLARD.
No idea what CLARD stands for,
I think it stands for *boring!*
It wasn't all bad though,
We made a castle out of the books and folders,
We called them CLARD castles.
We had pencil fights over the top of them
And I rolled my pencil sharpener down a track made out of rulers.

The bell rings again and it's dinner time.
The dinners were weird coloured slop
That tasted like dead animals.
More wars between Year 3 and 4,
In pain, and the dinner ladies
Blowing the whistle to call years to the dinner hall.
We had to stay perfectly still,
Even if we were in mid-air.

Then afternoon lessons,
Completely random,
Rubber fights,
Pencil fights,
. . . ruler fights.
Science that has no experiments,
Art with no drawing.
Weird.
Then home time at 3.30,
Hoopla!
We all run home,
Wishing we didn't have to come back in the morning.

Adam Dickinson (12)
Tottington High School, Bury

The Environment

Factories and cars,
Polluting the air,
Litter left in heaps,
On the streets everywhere.

Forests cleared,
Animals hurt,
Fish die in waters,
That have turned into dirt.

People drop litters,
Everywhere,
Wherever they want,
They don't care.

But if we use bins,
And recycle every day,
We can change the world,
In lots of ways.

Becky Foulkes (12)
Tottington High School, Bury

In Mrs Stewart's Class

You could play in the sandpit
Until your turn was over
Then Mrs Stewart would gently say
'Come sit with me, children, for a story'
After the story lots of children
Ran down the corridor
Break time

At break you could play anything
Skipping, tig, hide-and-seek or make-believe
Every child in the yard
Happy, smiling, laughing
You could eat or drink anything
Fruit, orange juice, sweets, milk
Then the sound of a whistle echoed in the air
It was over
Your fifteen minutes of freedom

In the classroom
You looked around
Plastic pots on the window sill
Each one contained a tiny plant
One of them was yours

Mrs Stewart gave out paper
It was as white as snow
And as smooth as a baby's bum
She said draw yourself and gave out a gentle smile
You loved Mrs Stewart
Because Mrs Stewart loved you
Stickers were handed out
Yours was a gold smiley face
Then it was dinner

You held someone's hand as you walked down the hall
You were led into the cloakroom
And told to find your lunch box
You walked down the endless lines of coats
Until you came to your sticker
It was a bunch of grapes and there underneath
Was your lunch box
Then you went into a huge room
You were scared
Then you saw Mrs Stewart
You were safe again
Her warm glow reminded you of your mother
As you ate your lunch.

Then you were outside
You got to ride a trike
On the pretend track
It was fantastic!
Before you knew it
The best day of your life was gone
Home again
Waiting for the next day to come.

Sophie Mather (13)
Tottington High School, Bury

Environment Poem

E veryone uses the environment
N ewspapers, water, space and air
V ery polluting one might say
I n America, car fumes and tons of carbon dioxide
R ussia produces poisonous gases
O n Scoutmoor, wind farms cause arguments
N o one wants them
M any thousands of views spoiled
E lectricity makers spinning, helping save us
N orth, east, south, west
T he world needs saving, the world needs you.

Andrew Fairclough (13)
Tottington High School, Bury

Recycling

Take a look around yourself,
While you're in the street,
Cans and litter everywhere,
All around your feet.

People don't bother,
They just walk past and ignore,
Like an object that's invisible,
Like a beggar on the floor.

There's one way we can solve this,
By simply using a bin,
Put different things in suggested containers,
You can recycle anything.

Recycle bins are usually local,
So why not walk or ride?
Help to save the environment
And help the animals survive.

It's up to you to make a stand,
To stop the litter lout,
To call a sudden halt to this wasteful act,
Like a boxer in a knockout bout.

Rachel Thomas (13)
Tottington High School, Bury

Litterman

I am a litterman,
I litter all around,
If I've got a bit of rubbish,
I drop it on the ground.
My surroundings are a dump,
I litter here and there,
That's the way I like it,
If you don't, well I don't care.
That chocolate bar was nice,
But where do I put the foil?
I'll drop it in a flower bed
And hide it in the soil.
They say I am so lazy,
That I should set a good example,
But all I do is drop a bit of litter,
That, for me, is ample.
Every now and again,
A bit of litter on the ground,
I just can't see how that
Could stop the world from going round.

Imagine if everyone said that.
Don't drop litter.

Robert Dennis (13)
Tottington High School, Bury

My Primary School Memories

The whistle sounded like a steam train,
Loud and sharp, coming to take us all into lessons.

The teacher sat us all on the carpet
So she could overlook us all.
We called her Miss James. Simple. Easy to remember.
She wore colourful leggings, matching her garden,
Purple pansies and pink primroses,
On a bed of minty green grass.

She came round to our tables,
Blue, red, green and yellow.
I was in red, letter box red. Block red. Plain red. Red.
We had first pick of collage materials.
Pastels, paints or crayons.
We had to have messy paints.
We were the good group.

The school photograph.
You brushed your hair and carefully placed
Your blue and white headband on your head.
You sat on the cold, hard, grey school chair,
Nervous about your pale blue appearance.
The strange man told you to smile, so you did.
Your tiny, white teeth shone through your pink lips.
A flash. It was done.

Sports day.
You wore your favourite Spice Girls T-shirt.
You waited quietly for your race. The obstacle race.
The whistle went and you were off.
You galloped to your hoop and threw it over your ponytail.
You sprinted to the bean bags
And smashed one onto your bat.
You half ran, half walked.
You could see your teacher smiling at the end.
You ran towards her. You had won!

The last day of school arrived.
You carried your baby-pink Barbie camper van under your arm.
It was your last day at Barnwood Primary.
Miss James gave you a card and wished you good luck.
You thanked her and ran outside to play with your friends
For the last time. Year 2 dawned . . .

Hannah Price (13)
Tottington High School, Bury

Put The World Right

Polluting the air,
But no one will care.
More people are giving birth,
Which affects the population of the Earth.

The Earth is being destroyed
And everyone's annoyed.
We need a solution,
Which will stop this revolution.

The Earth is too hot,
Sizzle will it not?
This is why, we need to try
And stop this before we all die.

Use a bike, or take a hike
And see what the world will be like.
This isn't right, we need to put up a fight,
Then we might see sight
And the world will be right!

Kirstie Bailey (13)
Tottington High School, Bury

Primary School

The first thing you saw was the cloakroom,
That looked like it had been hit with a boom!
Coats and bags
Were left in rags
And caked in mud from our shoes

Then into the classroom you went,
And then from there you were sent,
To take your seat
And tackle the feat
Of keeping your yellow books neat

Then out of the window you peer,
The teacher knows like a mystic seer,
She gives you a fierce glare
As you sit and you stare
And act like you knew what she said

Then the bell tolls
And the whole class rolls
Out of class in a chaotic style,
You play for a while,
Then go back inside
As the whole class returns like high tide

The computers were,
With a beep and a whirr,
Like portals out of this world,
We thought they were great,
But it was our sorry fate
To use them at only wet break.

James Kidd (13)
Tottington High School, Bury

In Year 6

You could see:
The large, red pots in the middle of the table,
Like huge bricks.
Your desks,
Looking like big, wooden mouths on legs.
The wall, with peeling, old green paint,
Like a crumbly, cracked witch's face.
The chalk board, like pen and paper,
Only white on black, not black on white.

You could smell:
Old glue when we were painting,
Like an old rubber.
The plastic smell of Sellotape and Blu-Tack,
Like a new toy.
The wet coats when it had been raining,
Like a weaving, old canal.
Dust, like a very old building.
Chalk, like a hot, dry day
And the scent of a pencil,
Quickly shaved to carry on with a dictation.

You could hear:
Mr Copeland booming across the room,
Like a foghorn.
The children shrieking at each other,
Like budgies arguing
And children constantly walking about,
Sounding like applause.

You felt:
Hot because of the June sun.
Tired, because of staying up too late
And impatient, waiting for home time.

Edward Robson (13)
Tottington High School, Bury

The Gloomy Days

Here we are.
In the hellhole again.
We hang our bags up on the neat pegs.
You can hear the laughing in the playground,
Which sounds like feeding time at the zoo,
With the elephants strolling around
And the small cubs scared and worried.
The bell goes.
It sounds like Big Ben's chimes that have got drunk.
The cookie monster comes to see us into the dark, gloomy classroom.
He stands with his head up high,
He looks like a squirrel with no hair.
We walk.
We walk into the classroom that has the walls painted
Like a child's ice cream that has been dropped on the floor!
The desks remind you of the Victorian times.
Here comes the air freshener,
It was like a bright summer's day at first,
Then it was choking you.
You could smell the chips,
Which smelt like greasy oven fat,
That hadn't been cleaned for years!
Then comes the clashing of the cutlery,
Which sounded like the recorder group!
The day dawns with the clouds standing heavy.
The same old dull bell goes,
The one you will hear tomorrow
And the next day and the next!

Hayley Driver (13)
Tottington High School, Bury

Primary School

Your ears are enchanted
By the bell's gentle melody. A slice of crisp toast,
Golden butter draped delicately on top.
Jack Frost was left behind
In the stinging bitterness he created.
Miss Smith welcomed you
Like the blissful days of summer.

Princesses, princes, fairies and wizards,
You could see them all, floating high above the clouds
On your magic carpet. Then you could create your own.
Miss Smith always there to guide your spidery characters.
That for an hour, then a luscious red apple,
Always unintentionally suspicious of its notorious reputation.

Huge blocks of colour hung off the wall,
Like huge palettes of bright, exciting paint.
Soft feathers, shimmering sequins, rustling tissue paper,
All as bright and as colourful as a glistening rainbow,
Stored momentarily in their labeled trays.
Then you could become a snake,
Shedding your once white PVA skin.

The bell sung once . . . *dinner time!*
Children lined up like troops eager to enter battle.
A bright red tray glowed in the afternoon sun.
Chicken dinosaurs roared and the potato smiles
Grinned as they were dipped in the lukewarm beans.
Then delicious cake, a creamy chocolate filling,
Smothered in lovely thick custard that flowed
Like a waterfall in your throat.

You adored school!

Naomi Tod (13)
Tottington High School, Bury

Reception Class Haikus

The tables like sweets,
Coloured and hexagonal,
Almost good to eat.

Detox, pee and milk,
Sickly mixed and smelt like bins,
Made you want to puke.

Paints by the window,
Multicoloured butterflies,
Flapping in a field.

A small, blue carpet,
No, a sea of fluff and hair,
Lying at the back.

Great, big, rude noises,
Thundering across the room,
Along with laughter.

A sink by the door,
Blocked up with paper and paint,
A swirling whirlpool.

Wet, cold, plastic coats,
Smelling like the rude noises,
But not as sickly.

The chatter of kids,
Sounded just like the market,
With the pretend shop.

The nice, wet, sand pit,
It felt just like a warm beach,
Just without seaweed.

This is reception,
The class with smiling faces,
Like lots of bright sparks.

Luke Aspinall (13)
Tottington High School, Bury

Untitled

You could choose your own sticker,
An apple, a grape, a bus.
Then you'd hang your coat up.
Next a story.
You could eat porridge with Goldilocks,
Chop down a beanstalk,
Run away from a wolf.
Then a drink.
More fruit.
A cup of fun, a glass of laughter.

The room was open to you,
Like an unlimited sweet shop.
Baskets spilling.
Lego, drawers crammed with crayons.
The smell of dust, like an attic.
The taste of disinfectant, like a hospital.
The feel of safety, just like home.
Next a break.
A necklace of a bell.

Finally, your cage was open.
The animals set free.
It was wild and loud.
You could ride a bike,
Drive around the pretend road,
Pretending to be a police lady.
And another bell, a key to lock you back in.
But it was OK. There was another story.

Then your mum came.
You got your coat from your sticker.
Mrs Stenton said goodbye.
You did too.
You ran home impatiently,
Desperate to sleep,
So you could wake up and get back to school.

Leanne Savery (13)
Tottington High School, Bury

In Mrs Fountain's Class

The classroom was as blue as the sea,
The tables were the seashells scattered about on the beach
In wonderful colours.
You could hear the children playing,
Having as much fun as when you are on holiday.

The next classroom was as loud as a big brass band
At the circus.
Mrs Fountain was as fun and lovable as a clown.
The reading area was as bouncy and comfortable
As a landing mat under a trapeze.

The corridor was as long and bendy as a snake,
The chalk board was as black as a spider.
The flowers were as colourful as a chameleon,
The cacti were as green and spiky as a spiky caterpillar.

It was great being there,
It was fun.
I was happy,
She was amazing.

Jessica Brindle (13)
Tottington High School, Bury

Dragon Books

Blue books, brown snakes
Wizards make magical mistakes
Fighting the guardian of fire
Wanting big treasure that they desire
Angry reptile set out flames
Playing really dangerous games
Glittery horns set out a wrath
Wizards use harmful staffs.

Paul Edwards (12)
Wareham Middle School, Wareham

House Of Gloom

In the house, scary things belong,
The dark corridors are very long.
I'm careful when I open each door,
I never know what's going to come through the floor.
The sound of bats screech in your ear,
It's the loudest thing you could ever hear.
The ghosts stand out in the moonlight,
They are looking angry and ready to fight.
If I reach out as far as I can,
I might find the body of a man.
The big spiders crawl up my back,
I can't see because it's pitch-black.
I curled up in a ball and quietly said,
'All I wish is that I could be in my bed.'

Sarah Thomas (12)
Wareham Middle School, Wareham

The Haunted Nursery

51 Bell Street,
Where a young girl died,
She won't come out,
All she does is hide.

The chalk board now writes
All on its own,
The character of the writer
Will never be shown.

For the girl now cries,
In the bathroom locked,
Beware, don't go in,
Your way out will be blocked!

Michael Alberry (12)
Wareham Middle School, Wareham

Footie

Spiraling out of control
As the crowd go wild
When they score a goal
Throwing everything they have
Into this one game
Will they take home the cup
And take home fame?

Shouting and screaming
One minute to go
Can they win this
It's their time to glow
Pass midfield and pass centre
Ten seconds left, he shoots
But will it enter?

Danielle Burbidge
Wareham Middle School, Wareham

Football Grounds

At old football grounds
There are spooky sounds
Like the moaning wind
And the trickling rain
Around rolls an old football
There's an old, damaged burger stall
A magazine flies around
Making a rustling sound
These are the spooky sounds
At old football grounds.

James Drane (13)
Wareham Middle School, Wareham

The Griffin

Griffins are friendly beasts,
But they like to have a feast,
On the teachers in your school,
That's the one thing that makes them drool.

Griffins eat teachers, tall and short,
They even eat when you're being taught!
So send griffins to the staffroom,
They will eat until they need the bathroom.

Let all griffins into your school,
They will eat teachers all,
So if you want to become a teacher,
A griffin might just come and eat ya.

Harry Ward
Wareham Middle School, Wareham

The Good Fairy

I grant you some wishes,
Morning or night,
Wherever you are,
I'll give you a fright.

I like to come up,
In your world I stay,
Because back under,
I cannot play.

That is the tale,
Of the good fairy,
She'll see you soon,
If you play fairly.

Kara Birch
Wareham Middle School, Wareham

The Blackest Gift

There's an evil little fairy there in the woods
Eyes like raging fire
Skin as pale as chalk
Claws as sharp as knives
And hair as soft as feathers.
She can look really sweet
But don't let that fool you
For if you get too close she might even kill you

There's a sad little creature
Down by the lake
Eyes like shining pearls
And tusks like spears.
He wouldn't hurt a fly
But people just can't see
That he acts just like you or me.

Sophie Bellingham (13)
Wareham Middle School, Wareham

The Bottom Of My Garden

Down at the bottom of my garden,
A raging river flows,
Down at the bottom of my garden,
Hardly any wildlife grows.
Down at the bottom of my garden,
The old wall falls down,
Down at the bottom of my garden,
There's endless groaning sounds.

Kieran Taylor
Wareham Middle School, Wareham

Love

Love is inexplicable
And can sometimes be painful
Your heart skips a beat
Which gives off a lot of heat

It's all about emotions
You feel like you've taken a potion
You're on air and flying
It's all on trust but no spying

Love is like poison
It spreads all over your body
Until you're infected
When you meet a person they inspected.

April Parslow (13)
Wareham Middle School, Wareham

Footprints

Think of the footprints in the sand,
Think of the footprints on the land.

Big, small, thin or wide,
They're all the same in someone's eyes.

Think of the footprints next to you,
Think of the footprints behind you.

Long, short, fat or wide,
They're all the same in God's own eyes.

Gabriella Mytton-Mills (12)
Wareham Middle School, Wareham

Falling In Love!

How could I know when I first met you
I would fall in love,
'Cause out of the blue you came my way.
So lost for words,
Didn't know what to say,
It's a craving,
It felt like I was misbehaving
And that I was going crazy.
Only you could save me,
I was falling and I didn't stop.
A little bit wasn't enough,
I knew I was falling,
Try as I might I couldn't hide.
When you came,
You unlocked all I had inside,
Like a piece of puzzle that slots so fine,
You came into my life and you made it right.
But now it's not just my heart you're stealing,
You know all there is to know,
You've seen inside my soul,
You're on my mind and I'm in love!

Roxanne Baker (13)
Westwood St Thomas' School, Salisbury

You

The sun is hot,
The sun is bright,
The sun goes down at night.

The moon is white,
The moon is bright,
The moon goes down in the morning light.

The sky is blue,
The sky is you

You are my whole world plus two!

Danielle Cotsell (14)
Westwood St Thomas' School, Salisbury

Life

Life is full of wonderful things
Like every time the doorbell rings
You wonder who is standing there
Or perhaps a grisly bear
Then you have friends
But every time you break up
You always make amends
You have short ones, tall ones
Fat ones, thin ones
Each having 206 bones
From the day since you were born
Since you died not one person didn't mourn
Not a day went by when you weren't unloved
And your voice was always loud
And never went unheard
Always quieter than a sheep escaped from a herd
Your secrets are a door with no key
Your clothes were never torn
When your time ends
All those love letters that still pend
Life is full of wonderful things.

Koby Waters (14)
Westwood St Thomas' School, Salisbury

The Rose

My love,
He gave me a red, red rose,
But it pricked me with its thorn.
Ever since that prick,
He has drifted away,
Like a ship out to sea.
So beware the thorns of the red, red rose
And watch they don't take him away.

Holly Turner (14)
Westwood St Thomas' School, Salisbury

That Man By The Window

I walked through the door,
Of the small, small inn,
And right by the bar I saw the barmaid,
She was watching, watching the corner,
Who or what was she watching?
That man by the window?

It didn't feel right,
Staying in that inn,
So I left for the hotel down the road.
He followed me, he followed me!
I went to the room, he was there!
That man by the window!

I demanded to know who he was,
He just said, 'A friend.'
'What do you want?' I screamed at him.
'To take you home,' he told me.
He took off his cloak and I saw,
That the man by the window was my dad!

Brierly Keeton (14)
Westwood St Thomas' School, Salisbury

My Gran

My gran had cool hair
She treated me and my sister fair.

My gran was called Honey
Sometimes I would get confused and call her Mummy.

My gran and I were ever so close
Now she is the one I miss the most.

My gran said that she would love me for evermore
My gran isn't alive anymore.

Lisa Shearmon (14)
Westwood St Thomas' School, Salisbury

Best Friends

Laughing or crying
Whatever it be
My friends are there
They can depend on me!

Doesn't matter the situation
They will always be
My bestest friends
And mean the world to me.

Some are shy and quiet
Some are weird, crazy and mad
All of them are caring and fun
Even those can be bad!

Whenever I am sad
They will always be
The weirdest, craziest
Bestest friends to me!

Laura Stokes (14)
Westwood St Thomas' School, Salisbury

Untitled

When you left my life
It cut like a knife.

The days are slow
The nights are long.

You're here, you're there,
You're everywhere.

As you say a prayer
You feel you shouldn't dare
Because it doesn't seem fair.

Sophie Astley (14)
Westwood St Thomas' School, Salisbury

Mrs Blues Thinks I'm Listening . . .

Mrs Blues thinks I'm listening, but I'm not:
I am swimming with dolphins,
I am scuba-diving in the sea,
I've just seen a shark swim over my head,
I'm in the film 'Lord of the Rings',
Strider has just proposed to Arwen,
Someone suspicious has put my favourite flowers on my doorstep,
I'm the director for a brand new film,
I have a limousine,
My wedding dress is lilac,
I have fairy wings,
Oh no, everybody's gone!
What's the time?

Angelia Ferris (14)
Westwood St Thomas' School, Salisbury

Untitled

The new start, is my new beginning,
With a smile on my face, I'm hopefully winning.
No one knows who I am,
Or what I think, or what's my plan.

I don't know where the hell I'm going,
I'm scared to death, I hope it's not showing.
I'll give the world as good as it gets,
Forget the baddies and their threats!

Holly Clarke (14)
Westwood St Thomas' School, Salisbury

In My Mind Every Day

Our friendship was true
Trust me it will never end.

Your chips were the best
I would eat one and then the rest.

Our hearts sank when you were gone,
You were like a second mum.

Rest in peace, sadly missed by everyone,
I will never forget you.

You are in my mind every day,
You were the best and still are!

Delith Morton (13)
Westwood St Thomas' School, Salisbury

Remembrance

November is here again,
The 11th day that's what it said.
Poppies to remember the dead.
Green leaf and poppies red,
Full with happiness, with no sorrow,
Never knew what would happen tomorrow.

Now the war is over, with nothing in sight,
Poppies were woken that night.
The place will never be the same,
Many people, they all can be named.

Helen Grinter (14)
Westwood St Thomas' School, Salisbury

Wales

As red as Wales' rugby shirts
As blue as the bluebirds
As yellow as daffodils
As green as the valleys
As white as the top of Snowdonia
As black as the caves in Brecon
As grey as the castles
As pink as the house in St Fagan's
As brown as the Opera House
These colours make me proud to be Welsh.

Kenneth Marshall (17)
Woodlands Special High School, Cardiff

Rainbow Wales

As red as the dragon on our flag
As yellow as a daffodil in the garden
As pink as the house in St Fagan's museum
As green as leeks we eat
As orange as the sunset at the Gower
As purple as the bruises on the rugby players
As blue as the sky in summer
That's what Wales means to me.

Jonathan Bryant (18)
Woodlands Special High School, Cardiff